ON TARGET MARKETING

A Road Map to Driving a Stampede of Local Targeted Internet Leads to your Business!

Mike Driggers
&
Vince W Baker

INSTANT AUTHORITY

Special **FREE** Bonus Gift For **YOU!**

To help you stand out from the crowd
FREE BONUS RESOURCES for you at;
www.InstantAuthorityNow.com

Get your 3 FREE in-depth training videos sharing how you gain trust from prospective customers. This trust will lead to establishing you as an authority, increase web traffic, boost business sales and attract more referrals. You will also learn how to earn the respect in your industry which can lead to more lucrative partnerships.

www.InstantAuthorityNow.com

Copyright © 2014 by Mike Driggers, and Vince W Baker

All rights reserved. No part of this publication may be reproduced, distributed or transmitted in any form or by any means, including photocopying, recording, or other electronic or mechanical methods, without the prior written permission of the publisher, except in the case of brief quotations embodied in critical reviews and certain other noncommercial uses permitted by copyright law. For permission requests, write to the publisher, addressed "Attention: Permissions Coordinator," at the address below.

Mike Driggers and Vince W Baker/ IME Publishing Group
www.OnTargetMarketingGroup.com
www.IMEPublishingGroup.com

Warning—Disclaimer

Disclaimer and Terms of Use: The Authors and Publisher has strived to be as accurate and complete as possible in the creation of this book, notwithstanding the fact that they do not warrant or represent at any time that the contents within are accurate due to the rapidly changing nature of the Internet. While all attempts have been made to verify information provided in this publication, the Authors and Publisher assumes no responsibility for errors, omissions, or contrary interpretation of the subject matter herein. Any perceived slights of specific persons, peoples, or organizations are unintentional. In practical advice books, like anything else in life, there are no guarantees of income made. Readers are cautioned to reply on their own judgment about their individual circumstances to act accordingly. This book is not intended for use as a source of legal, business, accounting or financial advice. All readers are advised to seek services of competent professionals in legal, business, accounting, and finance field.

On Target Marketing/ Mike Driggers and Vince W Baker. —1st ed.
ISBN: - 978-0-9973034-1-4

CREATE A STAMPEDE OF LOCAL LEADS
"Share This Book"

Retail 24.95
Special Quantity Discounts

5-20 Books	22.95
21-99 Books	19.95
100-499 Books	15.95
500-999 Books	10.95
1,000 + Books	8.95

To Order Go To www.OnTargetMarketing.com

THE IDEAL PROFESSIONAL SPEAKERS FOR YOUR NEXT EVENT!

Any organization that wants to develop and grow their business to become "extraordinary" needs to hire Mike or Vince for keynote or workshop training!

TO BOOK MIKE OR VINCE TO SPEAK:

On Target Marketing Group
(925) 222-5037
www.OnTargetMarketingGroup.com

TheOTMGroup@gmail.com

DEDICATION

This book is dedicated to all the entrepreneurs that have an unwavering passion, a constant flow of ideas, the desire to be an expert, and a forward-looking approach to growing their business.

Lead generation in today's world is not just about trying to build sales; it's about building relationships that cultivate loyalty for long term sales.

Lead generation is just the start of the consumer's interest into your products or services. Your clients and customers want more; they want authenticity in their business relationships with you. A smart marketing strategy can be the difference between solidifying customer relationships or losing them.

The first step for an entrepreneur is knowing where to start and having a plan of action. This will help to establish you as an authority in your industry. We have written this book to help you establish authenticity and be the authority in your market.

Vince and Mike both know what it takes and this is why they have dedicated this book to you.

The Entrepreneur!

Table of Contents

Chapter 1: Introduction 1

Chapter 2: It All Begins With A Plan 9

Chapter 3: Explode Your Return on Investment 15

Chapter 4: Authority Marketing - The Power Of Positioning Yourself As An Expert In Your Industry 27

Chapter 5: Dominate Your Local Market 51

Chapter 6: How To Get A Stampede Of Targeted Leads To Your Website 65

Chapter 7: What Makes A High Converting Website? 89

Chapter 8: Strategic Online Sales Funnels – Building The Perfect Sales Funnel 101

Chapter 9: Mobile Marketing – How To Generate More Leads & Sales 123

Chapter 10: Working Smarter, Not Harder 139

Chapter 11: Putting It All Together 149

Chapter 12:` One Last Message 153

Author Bios 157

Special FREE Bonus gift for you 168

Since I have had the pleasure of working with Vince and Mike I have found them to be both professional and knowledgeable. They have proven to be a great resource when it comes to online marketing and business strategies. Their skill sets and strategies can absolutely drive traffic and conversions. They are very innovative in working with the online and offline business world. I would highly recommend them both if you are looking for internet marketing.

Chet Finley
Founder of the Business Builders Club

If you're a business owner or marketer and you're going to read a book about how to drive more leads and more sales- then why not learn from guys that have been there and done that! By working with Vince and Mike my company's been able to benefit in minutes from knowledge and advice that would otherwise taken me months to accumulate. Vince and Mike have the practical experience needed to write this book that gets straight to the core of what a business owner needs to know about Internet marketing in order to effectively grow sales. I highly recommend you read and apply it!

Stu Rosenbaum
CEO, US Merchant Systems, LLC

Vince Baker and Mike Driggers are true professionals and the ideal duo to coach fellow entrepreneurs on the topic of generating Local Targeted Leads for their businesses. Having worked with these gentlemen many times over the past year, I'm excited to see the results of their readers' efforts after applying the formulas outlined in this great read.

Brad Lewis
Co-Founder & CEO of Agora Advantage, Inc.

CHAPTER 1

INTRODUCTION

It may not come as a shock to you unless you've been out of touch with the business world for a while, but there has been a major shift in how to successfully market your local business.

These days so many business owners are scratching their heads trying to figure out why their leads, customers or sales have dropped off and what they can do about it. Well, the good news is that this book will answer this for you.

You see, the shopping habits of consumers changed in alignment with economic conditions, technology and customer reviews. Which means, tried, tested and proven marketing strategies of the past no longer work.

The reality is the marketing techniques many local businesses used to depend on to reach their market in the past simply don't have the same impact. This means Yellow Page ads, newspapers and other types of hardcopy advertising are becoming more and more outdated. This is because the ads do not get the same amount of exposure they once received. They also don't carry the shelf life of internet marketing. Yellow pages were the number one source of advertising for the business before invention of the internet. In fact, do you know where your copy of the Yellow Pages is now?

These days, people are looking more and more to the internet to find information about the services, products and reviews they use every day. Additionally, they're searching not only locally, but they're searching nationally and internationally too. However, to be successful with this selling trend on the internet you have to have a proven *on target strategy*.

This brings up an interesting question: Do you know your customer-base, or are you struggling to grow your marketing share by using outdated numbers and statistical information from years past?

If you want your business to reach new customers in the current market environment, then you need to wake up, because while you were sleeping your competition's market power went global!

Your business name and your product or service must be where your customer-base is searching for your products or services. It doesn't do any good to have a billboard in the desert. Your business presence and advertisement plan must have a targeted strategy in the heart of the most trafficked areas.

The most trafficked area in this day and age is the internet. To be highly successful you need to be found in places where your customers are searching for your industry goods or services. The easier it is to find your business on the Internet, the more revenue you're going to generate from sales. Translation: *The results are going to show up as big bucks on your bottom-line! It is that simple.*

What many business owners don't realize is this means setting up your business with an online store-front that is open 24/7 to anyone who wants to visit. We call this your website. However, your website in today's marketplace has to be more than just an online brochure.

Your website must act as the hub with many spokes pointing to and from high trafficked sites such as YouTube, Facebook, Twitter, Google, Yahoo, Bing, Yelp and many other popular websites and business directories.

This small thinking, still in the box approach just doesn't cut it anymore. You must think of the Internet as a powerful marketing tool that can really help your business grow. Yes, grow, as long as it follows some basic online marketing principles. These principles can help you convert browsers to leads and buyers.

As more and more businesses catch on to the immense power of the Internet to help them, more businesses will boost their bottom-line profits. Result: There is an increase in businesses throwing up websites on the Internet to try and get in on the action.

The downside of this though is most fail miserably, because they put little to no thought behind their website. However, their competitors (who use a variety of specific online marketing techniques), stand out from the crowd and do extremely well.

Your website needs to be *search engine friendly*. Your website will also have to be effective in gaining new business or repeat business.

Today, because of the ever increasing number of businesses wanting to get found on the Internet, unless you apply specific Search Engine Marketing Strategies and Internet Marketing Campaigns to your website it probably won't get very many visitors to it; which means you won't get much business.

Getting business from the Internet is an ever changing medium that even Internet Marketing Experts have to work extremely hard in order to keep up to speed.

Where does this leave the average business owner? It leaves them scratching their heads about what they need to be spending their marketing budget on to get leads, customers or sales from the Internet without taking away from their bottom line. Without a targeted online strategy thousands of dollars can be wasted in places that will not bring in the desired results. This book will help your company with an on target internet strategy to turn this around in your favor. Business owners have their hands full managing staff and keeping customers happy, coupled with the day-to-day business operations. When you add in the super fast-paced world of online marketing, and toss in business owners trying to figure out what to do, then you're left with business owners who don't know where to begin.

What exactly is Internet Marketing?

Internet marketing can be broken down into the different ways your business finds people who are searching for products or services online and turning them into customers. But that's not all; it's also about brand awareness; social proofing and developing a strategy that will help your business stand out from the ever increasing crowd trying to market their business online.

Ask yourself the following two questions. Then answer each one.

Look at the list below and ask yourself:

1. What do I know about each area on the list?
2. Do I know how each can help me dominate the Internet?
   - Organic Traffic (SEO)
   - Paid Traffic (PPC)
   - Social Media Traffic
   - Backlinks
   - Authority Marketing
   - Social Proof
   - Reputation Management
   - Website Conversion Strategies
   - Opt-in Forms
   - Squeeze Pages
   - Sales Funnels
   - Purpose of a Blog
   - Mobile Marketing
   - Business Directories
   - Content Optimization

Don't be alarmed if you answered --not much! This is expected.

The good news is by the time you have finished reading this book your understanding will be massively different. In fact, you'll know exactly what you need to do to market your business on the Internet. You'll also know how to cash in on this best advertising medium that has ever hit the marketplace.

To make it even clearer, what we love about using the Internet is it has the ability to drive a stampede of qualified leads to your virtual store-front, or as some call it *your 24/7, no-days-off, sales machine.* The fact is the return on investment (ROI) makes every dollar you spend on internet advertising virtually staggering.

We, personally, have seen a return as high as 47,000 percent ROI for email marketing campaigns. This is simply unheard of in most of the traditional TV, Radio, Billboards or print based advertising mediums we once relied on.

The point is clear, whether you make $2 for every dollar you spend on your marketing budget, or $1,000 for every dollar spent; the opportunity for your profits to soar and the opportunity for your business to boom is only limited by your knowledge and how quickly you apply it.

Allow us to give you an example; let's take an accountant that gets $8,000 a month in revenue from selling just 4 self managed superfunds a month from his website. That's $2000 a week from 1 product that he markets on his site. He also gets thousands of dollars a month in sales from new clients who sign-up for his accounting services.

We worked out the averages around 12,000% ROI on what he spends to get this one business off and running. He is using only 1 Internet marketing strategy called, SEO (Search Engine Optimization).

4 Keys to Online Marketing Success:

1) Develop an Online Marketing plan so your business can dominate the internet for your local area and be perceived as a trusted market leader.

2) Create the most effective ways to drive a stampede of free and paid qualified traffic to your site each and every day on auto-pilot.

3) Establish the essential elements to turn your website into a high-converting lead generation or sales machine.

4) Launch the best way to get any or all of your Internet Marketing done turnkey for you so you can focus on growing your business and doing what you do best.

In the next chapter we're going to focus on developing your plan.

CHAPTER 2

IT ALL BEGINS WITH A PLAN

The first place to start when looking at getting the best return on your investment for marketing online is your website.

Long gone are the days when you could simply upload a website that looks like a brochure and add some basic information and perhaps add a few meta-tags and hope to get a ton of business. *In fact, your website if not done properly could turn business away from you.* Also, gone are the "Presto" days when your website would end up getting found by the search engines. Just having a website presence is not enough.

These days your website needs to serve multiple purposes, while interacting with the rest of popular social media sites, video sites, search engines, review sites and business directories. But, the main focus should still remain congruent with your original goals of pulling more traffic to your website.

Let us explain. The purpose of a website can be defined as:

- Promotional
- Generate leads
- Build a database
- Sell products or services online
- Provide information
- Attract new clients
- Call attention to customer reviews
- Add value to existing clients (i.e. member's area)

Do you know how to achieve all of the above? If the answer is *no* to this question, than by using this book as a tool you can setup your website to achieve your goals and purposes.

The above list should be followed whether you have an existing website or you're considering a new website; otherwise your website will never achieve it's true potential and it will cost you time and money in the process.

Here's another super important tip:

"Websites Need To Change As The Internet Evolves."

We don't know how many web owners we have come across that haven't looked at their website in years, let alone invested the time and energy to freshen it up and bring it more in alignment with current search habits or search engine compliance guidelines. Websites must have a fresh appeal to this new generation of internet users.

At a glance your potential customers will judge your business as established and trustworthy, or outdated and not up to speed with today's internet standards. It is imperative that your website is on the forefront of look, appeal and full of rich content to meet your goals. It takes less than two-tenths of a second for an online visitor to form a definitive opinion about your brand.

In today's market your website is usually the first place a prospect looks to find your products and services. On the average you can expect your website to generate 50% or more of your business either directly or indirectly. As a business owner you have to realize you may do a better job than your competitor, but business will be lost if customers searching the internet feel your competition is more trustworthy or better equipped to meet their needs. This can occur because of what is portrayed on your competitions website.

Remember:

It is all about how you tell your story effectively online to your customers that will make the difference of them doing business with you or your competition.

We have many business owners telling us, "Lately, 18-months ago" they "Got 90% of their business from walk-ins or referrals" and now they are "getting 90% of their business from the Internet."

The reality is the internet is constantly changing and evolving. If your website fails to keep up with the times it will quickly fall behind those that are adapting to change. The internet is a goldmine of business opportunity, but first you must know how to mine it. The websites that adapt and change will prosper, and those that don't will fail. You have to remember that most buyers will shop you out on the internet before they choose who they are going to buy from or do business with.

Everything you do affects your internet presence and internet sales of your product(s) or service(s). This includes from how your website looks to what content you use, customer reviews and right down to how easy it is to update your chosen keywords. All parts make up the whole, resulting in your website becoming and staying one of your most powerful marketing tools.

These days your website can become your #1 source of new business, as well as, being a highly cost effective way of getting past customers to return, buy more and refer friends.

What Makes Up A Good Website?

Here are 17 Tips to optimizing your website:

1. Be clear about what you want your visitors to do.
2. Take advantage of all of your customer reviews.
3. Make good use of powerful videos.
4. Have strong calls to action.
5. Make it easy for your customers to find you.
6. Feature your unique selling proposition.
7. Make sure all the important information is "above the fold" of your website.

8. Provide additional conversion paths.

9. Shorten contact forms.

10. Get rid of unnecessary text or links.

11. Use a simple website design and layout.

12. Make your words and images count.

13. Convey trust and authority.

14. Make it easy for your customers to contact you.

15. Interact with your main social media sites.

16. Know Your Stats.

17. Keep it simple and not overly busy.

Today, local business owners are in a hungry marketplace. They need more work. They need to attract more clients. They need to adapt to the changing economy, or more specifically, they need to know how to reach the market as it is changing. Understanding the change in consumer buying habits and understanding and staying ahead of trends in consumer spending is essential to business survival.

Case in point:

One local business was spending $1,000 per month on *Yellow Page* advertising that cost more than the revenue it was bringing in. In fact, the business owner was so unimpressed with the lack of results from the Yellow Page ads, he cancelled his ad.

Now the business owner is left with an annual $12,000 budget for marketing, but doesn't know where to spend the allotted money. He knows he needs to focus more on the internet, but he isn't sure where to start. This business owner is like many other entrepreneurs.

The entrepreneurs of today realize the internet is the future. They know more than 2.6 Billion local searches are performed online every month. They know this number grows by more than 50% each year. In fact, 80% of people search online before they make a purchase.

They now prefer this type of searching over *Yellow Pages* or newspapers. Therefore, entrepreneurs know the need and urgency of getting online to promote their businesses in an effective way. Marketing online and being internet marketing savvy is this book's focus.

CHAPTER 3

EXPLODE YOUR RETURN ON INVESTMENT

The cost of effective online targeted marketing should never be measured by how much you spend but by how much successful revenue it brings in. Using internet marketing can easily result in an increase in sales of tens of thousands of dollars. This is amazing considering the sheer number of layoffs, crises, and more economic hardships people are facing in today's economy.

The old ways of doing things are broken and people must learn something new. Many people who thought they had retired are back to work and working hard in businesses. They are the people who can use an internet marketing plan to save their business and their livelihood.

When you put online marketing strategies to work, you are not only impacting your own business in a positive way; you are improving your local economy. More money is being spent locally. You don't need to downsize or do layoffs.

In fact, your business will grow, despite the economy because you are reaching those who are looking to buy from a business like yours. This is what effective marketing is all about!

Online marketing has the potential for massive returns on your investment. If you are not ready for your business to double or triple --stop reading now!

Interesting Statistics

The following statistics give you a glimpse of how people use the internet in their choice of businesses to to work with:

- 64% of U.S. Gross domestic product comes from local businesses.
- 93% of online experiences begin with a search engine
- Over 80% of search is done with Google.
- Places pages account for over 20% of Google search volume.
- Over 40% of mobile search is done via Google Maps.
- 2.3 million searches per second on the average occur on Google.
- Over 2.6 billion local searches are performed monthly and this number grows more than 50% each year.
- 98% of searchers choose a business that is on page 1 of the results they obtain from their search.
- 41% of clicks go to the #1 ranked site in a search.
- 12% of clicks go to the #2 ranked site in a search.

- 8.5% of clicks go to the #3 ranked site in a search.
- 77% of mobile users seeking information search primarily using search engines.
- 67% of all Internet users use social networking sites on a regular basis.
- 52% of consumers say that watching product videos makes them more confident in online purchase decisions.
- 92% of online users have more confidence in information found online than they do in anything from a sales clerk or other source.
- 88% of consumers trust online reviews as much as personal recommendations.
- 90% of customers say buying decisions are influenced by reviews.

These statistics prove the importance of prioritizing an online marketing strategy, getting to the top of the search results and maintaining your online reputation. You really can dominate the internet when you use these facts to guide your internet marketing campaign.

A Simple Internet Marketing Plan: Dominate the Internet

To make the changes to your online marketing methods there are a variety of things you should know.

- First, the potential to grow your business using online marketing is phenomenal, no matter what industry you are in. You just need to cultivate it.

- There are 7 extremely useful internet marketing techniques very few businesses are doing. Learn them and put them into practice and you will quickly outperform all your competitors (See Page 19).

- There is a simple online marketing plan you can follow to make sure you get all the tasks done to get to the top of the search results and get more new clients to your site.

- Before implementing your new marketing plan, take the time to thoroughly analyze what you are already doing. Then you'll know where to go from there. You'll have a baseline to measure against. Focus your internet campaign on only what matters.

- Make your tasks more reasonable by breaking them down. Start with the tasks that are one-time jobs, as they provide the foundation for your marketing plan. Then you'll have the pleasure of checking things off your list.

- When the one-time online tasks are completed, you should begin the tasks that repeat. These are long term commitments requiring monthly, weekly, or even daily attention.

- You should consider seeking out subcontractors for a portion of (or), the entire online marketing plan, simply for the sake of expediency and skill. There are many who can take on selected tasks to facilitate the process for you.

- You will conclude the implementation of your marketing plan with an increase in your business income.

7 Techniques Few Local Businesses Do:

While some people are using select internet marketing techniques to drive traffic to their site, others are doing none at all. They are *hoping for the best*. Using a wide variety of *tried and true* online marketing methods is the best way to see real results in your sales.

A great place to start is by opting to implement the 7 things practically no one is doing. These things produce serious results and should be used by every business owner with an internet presence. They include:

1. Latest News Feeds / Blog Updates
2. List Building
3. Free Reports / Giveaways
4. Video / YouTube
5. Basic SEO
6. Customer Reviews (Video Preferred)
7. Mobile Friendly Website

Let's go over each one on the list below.

1. Latest News Feed / Blog Updates:

Blogging creates a steady online presence that increases your chances of being at the top of search engine results for your keywords. By using a blog you can get content containing all your long-tailed keywords on the web. Search engines are built to find the most current and pertinent information for each subject being searched. Therefore, an updated blog will frequently stay at the top of search engines. Old and not currently updated sites are put at the bottom of search engines in most cases.

In addition, a blog allows you to build a following of customers and potential customers who are interested in what you share. 78% of people believe organizations that provide custom content want to build good relationships with them. It also creates social interaction and provides valuable feedback. This particular audience is ripe for being marketed to when your business is in a slump or keeping it from getting in a slump.

Remember:

Giving out free information about a subject matter on a blog makes you an expert in the eyes of potential customers, and customers want to buy from an expert they trust, like and know.

2. List Building

List building using auto-responder sequences is a tool which allows you to build an email list easily. It allows you to follow up with those on it. They are a set of standardized emails that are set up once. Then the necessary drip marketing contact is repeated every time a new individual opts into your email list. Emails are taken care of and go out automatically.

Auto-responders are an indispensable tool which saves time for you. They actually do some of the lead nurturing that is absolutely essential in demand marketing. They can be pre-written. This allows each new person added to your database to receive ongoing information for as long as you like. Just make sure your drip marketing to these opted in customers is not too little or too much. Find a happy medium.

Note:

It is easier to sell to an existing customer or someone in your data bank than to find a completely new customer. Your easiest sells could be found right in your existing data bank. You just have to harness a successful email campaign with an enticing offer to get them to buy again and again.

3. Free Reports/Giveaways

Offering free reports or giveaways to those who are interested is another of the under used tools in the online marketer's toolbox. Everyone loves getting something for free.

If you offer free reports or a free eBook (or even an online brochure on an area of interest in a specific field), you'll easily move visitors to your site to give you their email or other contact information. Interested individuals will give you their email information in exchange for a report, book or give away that actually provides useful information for them. Figure out what your potential customers may find useful or interesting and then give it to them for FREE. This allows you to capture their very important contact information.

4. Video

Video is the new version of blogs and articles. You can reach numerous customers and potential customers with this new hot online marketing tool. You can create a simple video from text or power point slides and add music, or record a video of actual products and services in use. Be sure to place videos both on your site and off site for maximum effectiveness.

Placing your videos on YouTube, Facebook and other popular sites will give you more internet presence. This can drive more traffic to your website. Statistics also show that visitors will stay on your website longer if there is interesting video present. Make sure the video is short, to the point, interesting, and with a call to action. Online audiences tend to have short attention spans, so make your videos powerful by following these guidelines. **To learn more about this topic download our FREE report "Video Marketing Excellence" at http://www.ontargetmarketing.com/video/sp**

5. Basic SEO

SEO is another tool that goes unused by those looking to promote their business online. It is simply making sure your website is as appealing as possible to the spiders that crawl the internet collecting information for search engines. This includes strategic use of keywords, backlinks and more. Backlinks are incoming hyperlinks from one web page to another website. Backlinks are believed to be one of *the* most important search engine ranking factors.

Many businesses pay a lot of money to have someone create a fancy looking website for them, but it is simply not search engine optimized, so it will never get ranked in the search engine results.

Without the strategic use of keywords, a significant number of links to their site will be lost. Also, the removal of sluggish things like Flash and music can make the difference between a website achieving a top ranking. Also, surveys show a one-second delay in page response can result in a 7% reduction in conversions.

6. Testimonials/Reviews

Customer reviews are a great way to build social proof right on your website. These days' reviews can have the power to make or break a business. It stands to reason the more positive customer reviews you have on your site, the more instant credibility your business warrants. This new generation of customers wants to know what the online community thinks about your company before they are ready to do business with you. On a side note, when dealing with reviews from a site like Yelp make sure you respond to any negative reviews. People understand that things can happen in business and when you show you care and handle any negative experience the customer had with your company in a positive way it can restore and maintain your online reputation. But if you don't stay on top of customer service you will suffer the consequences of negative online reviews and if left unchecked it could quickly get out of hand. Too many negative reviews can greatly hinder the flow of online traffic to your website. It can also greatly hinder online customer's desiring to do business with your company.

We have found video customer reviews carry far more weight than their text based cousins. Some customers feel that written reviews can be fabricated. Now a days if you have an iPhone or Smartphone you can do a video customer review at *point of sale* or completion of a service. We have used this with great success and it helps massively with converting new clients. Also having these video reviews on your website gives you the opportunity to have your customers selling for you 24/7.

Another way to use these same videos is by placing them in your social media posts. By doing this you will create a viral effect of likes and shares where others will see the positive reviews of your business throughout the social media world. These same videos will also create backlinks to your website (as we discussed earlier in the Basic SEO section and further on in the book) these backlinks give you credibility in the search engines that you want.

7. Mobile Friendly Website

Mobile browsing and searches are now happening more than desktop searches. Google's recent algorithm change means your site will drop significantly in search results or may not even show up if it is not mobile friendly. Don't get left behind! 82% of Smartphone users turn to their smart devices to help them make a product or service decision.

You really are shooting yourself in the foot if your website is not mobile friendly. A shrunk version of your website makes it difficult for mobile browsers to view or navigate. It ultimately will cost you in lost business. Make sure you personally look at your website from multiple smart phones or tablets. Different websites behave differently on various devices. This is important in our world today because more and more shoppers are using their smart phone or tablet when shopping on the go.

It is also a good idea to look how your website interacts on different web browsers such Google Chrome, Safari, Internet Explorer, and Firefox.

By putting in place the seven marketing plans above (that few are using), you'll easily and profitably set your website apart from most of your competitors. Your search engine results will begin to quickly climb. You will find more and more customers are "stumbling across" your website. You know you have reached your goal when you hear your customers say, "Everywhere I look online I see you!"

Here is another super important tip:

Study your online competition!

Never be afraid to study your competition. It's worth your while to see what they are doing or not doing. Knowing what deals they are offering and what the local community thinks about them is very important information when you are strategizing your online campaign. Why reinvent the wheel if they have found something effective that works. Maybe they are offering a better deal than you are. Or, why make the same mistakes they made. Learn from their mistakes so as not to make the same. You can easily achieve these goals by just reading or listening to their customer reviews, looking at their website, or doing a search on Google for their company. You will be surprised what you find by researching your competition out online.

CHAPTER 4

Authority Marketing- The Power Of Positioning Yourself As An Expert In Your Industry

People have always looked up to experts and authority figures, seeking them out for advice and following their recommendations. The word of an established authority weighs heavy for anyone who's trying to make some sort of decision, be it something personal or something they're looking to buy. By positioning yourself as an expert you can grow your business faster with more impact than your competition.

Becoming a well-known niche expert is something that can be immensely useful, not to mention profitable. People follow, trust and buy from experts. So what makes up an expert?

There are 3 things that make you an expert:

1. You have lived, breathed, and experienced your niche. A good example of this would be Bill Gates.

2. You have researched, been trained in or educated in a niche and now you train and educate others in that particular niche. Good example would be Dr. Oz or Dr. Phil who are both experts in their field.

3. You stand on the shoulder of giants. You interview all the experts in your niche. A good example of this would be Napoleon Hill the Author who wrote the book Think and Grow Rich in 1937 after researching the wealthiest men in the world and has sold over 70 million copies worldwide. The book has been translated into multiple languages.

By establishing yourself and your company as an expert you can drive tons of leads to your website. These leads can quickly turn into buyers when they see you as number #1 or a leader in your field. While everyone's path will be different, there are still many practices you should try to follow to maximize your chances of becoming an established authority in your field.

Why It's Important

In our daily lives we're constantly bombarded with people and ads telling us what to do, what to think and what to buy. Thankfully we're usually able to filter out information that we deem irrelevant or not trustworthy. We don't listen to just anyone. If a random person on the street told you he's going to invest $10,000 in a specific stock you'd probably wish him good luck and count yourself lucky that you're not the one gambling your money away on the stock market. But, if that person was Warren Buffett you'd probably be on the phone, calling a stock broker two seconds after the conversation ended. Why is that?

It's really simple: Warren Buffett is a Wall Street authority. Over the years he's built a reputation that makes people see him as an expert investor. You know he's the real deal, and if he was to give you a top secret, insider stock tip you'd probably listen to every word he had to say.

The same is true in any other field. The word of a reputable expert is always treated like gold, whether that expert is a plumber, a doctor or a personal development guru. And, it's the person who's put in the effort with personal branding that is most likely to achieve that expert status.

Say you were to launch an SEO marketing firm. Selling your services would be a lot easier if you were well-known and highly regarded within the SEO industry. Who do you think people would rather hire? The guy with 10,000 Twitter followers who consistently delivers ground-breaking SEO case studies, or the "nobody" who's been working quietly behind the scenes for 20 years, never sharing his techniques with anyone?

Even if they're on the same skill level, and have both had major success in their field, it's safe to assume that the first guy is well ahead in terms of authority and therefore much more likely to gain the business of people looking for an SEO expert.

Establishing yourself and your company as an authority on the internet will build the trust and credibility you need to drive high levels of traffic to your website. When people view you as a true authority in your field it will enable you to quickly build the rapport you need to turn a lead into a buyer.

Benefits Of Becoming An Authority

The benefits of establishing yourself as an authority in your field are numerous. When done right it's almost like a real life "cheat code" that puts you in a position where opportunity knocks at every turn.

Reasons Why You Should Try To Become An Authority In Your Niche

Practically every niche in existence has its own set of experts and authorities who get to enjoy the respect and admiration of the community. No doubt being an authority comes with a range of perks and benefits, and it's no wonder that so many strive to reach that level. If you've been considering giving it a shot, but you're still not convinced it's worth all the hard work required, here is a short list of some of the advantages that may aid you in making a decision:

1. Opportunity will knock on your door regularly

Being an authority means that people will want to work with you, utilizing your knowledge, fame and network to maximize the potential of their projects. This also means that you'll get plenty of chances to embark on joint ventures, or even just acting as an adviser but still getting a cut of the profits. It will be up to you to pick and choose among the projects offered to you, meaning you can focus on whatever suits you at the moment.

2. You'll always be invited

Every time there's a big event in your niche you can count on an invitation landing in your inbox. Most likely you'll be invited to many more events than you could possibly find the time to attend, both as a guest and maybe even a keynote speaker. You can also count on getting the VIP treatment wherever you go!

3. People will buy your products

If you've built up a reputation as an authority in your niche, and you were to one day start selling your own line of products, you can bet that people will be lining up ready to buy from you. All the trust you've built over the years means no one will be doubting the quality of your products, whether they're informational or physical. This is one of the most profitable paths to take once you've reached authority status, and it's no wonder you see so many authorities in all kinds of niches going this route.

4. People will trust your word

As an authority your word will be treated like gold. Even if you have an opinion that people disagree with, they'll still respect it because you are, after all, the authority. If anyone should know, it's you. Don't expect everyone to always agree with you though - even when you're an undisputed authority there will always be people who think of things differently and that is ok.

As an unknown nobody, voicing an unpopular opinion means

being instantly written off as ignorant. That's not the case when you're an authority. While people may not necessarily agree with you in everything you say, you can bet that they will at the very least respect your opinion. After all, you've spent years learning all the little ins-and-outs of your niche, and it seems unlikely that you would be plain ignorant about it.

5. You will gain a loyal following

You will gain a loyal following that take all your recommendations to heart. If you were to recommend a specific product you can bet that many of these followers will buy it, trusting your word that it's something that they could benefit from. Just look at what happens when a celebrity doctor endorses a new diet product on TV - instantly it starts selling in the millions, just based on the *exposure + authority figure* formula.

6. Your network will grow effortlessly

As an unknown nobody trying to get started building a network can be difficult and time-consuming. If you haven't got much to bring to the table it will be a very slow process. Everyone wants to network with those higher up on the ladder than themselves, ensuring they stand to gain something from it. It therefore follows that when you're at the top of the ladder, everyone will want to connect with you. You won't have to make any effort yourself, but you can just sit back and build your network passively.

7. You have the power of the whole community at your disposal

When you're at the top of the food chain in a niche, getting everyone under you to rally towards a common cause becomes fully doable. Say you get an idea to put on an event - all you have to do is reach out to the community and you'll most likely get all the help you need.

8. It will be easier for you to make money

As an established authority it will be easier than ever to make money. People will be fighting for a chance to work with you. Say you're a big authority in the fitness niche, having built up a large following and a solid reputation. In a normal, average week you may be contacted by people who want to pitch you their product ideas for joint ventures, people who offer you money to endorse their products, invitations to speak at events and countless other things.

9 Recommendations You Should Follow If You Want To Be Recognized As An Authority

If you want people to see you as an authority you need to carry yourself like one. People have certain expectations of authority figures, and unless you live up to them you'll risk losing your authority status eventually. Here are some of the most important things to keep in mind:

1. Be a leader

This one is a given. Authority figures should be leaders who aren't afraid to take the initiative and lead by example. What this means in practice depends on the niche and situation, but the key is to never act like a follower. People should follow you, not the other way around. To do this you need to carry yourself with authority.

2. Help others

A great way to cement your authority status is taking every opportunity you get to help others who need it, even if you don't benefit directly from it yourself. Every time you get a chance to help someone out - take it! Even if there is no apparent upside for you to do so. This is perfect for creating lifelong, loyal fans that will stop at nothing to return the favor in the future. Helping people without asking for anything in return is an excellent way to forge new relationships and gain a loyal following. You can bet that the people you help will be telling all their friends what a helpful, friendly and knowledgeable person you are, further cementing your authority status.

3. Go the extra mile

If there's one thing that truly helps when trying to become an authority figure, it's going the extra mile with everything you do. If you're blogging, strive to make every post a masterpiece. If you're on Twitter, be more active and put out better tweets than your competitors.

Look at what other, established authorities in your niche are doing, and work harder than them. Go the extra mile. It will always pay off!

4. Be social

You cannot become an authority without knowing and interacting with people in your niche. Whether it's offline or online on social networks, making an effort to be social and continually make new friends and contacts is one of the most powerful things you can do to make sure your authority status will remain today and in the future. All the connections you make have the potential to help you and stick up for you, so never pass up an opportunity to make a new friend!

5. Network regularly

The more people you know who can vouch for your expertise and help spread the word about your endeavors, the better. You should always be on the lookout for networking opportunities, whether it's online or in real life. Don't be too quick to rule out potential new connections either, as you never know who or what may be helpful in the long run. A person who may not be of much practical use to you now could very well end up being the number one contributor to your success in the future. Embrace every networking opportunity and don't risk missing out on potential benefits.

6. Don't be afraid of controversy

When you're trying to build up your authority status your natural instinct may be to shy away from controversy in order to not alienate anyone. Some people fear being controversial, but as an authority you should in fact embrace it. A little bit of controversy can do wonders for your personal brand. People are drawn to controversy and there is no better chance to market yourself than placing yourself right in the middle of it. The thing to remember here is that not everyone has to agree with you. The key is recognizing chances to voice an unpopular (but right) opinion and going against the grain - that's when controversy can play into your hands. However, don't stir things up just to be controversial, that'll likely be counterproductive.

7. Take the initiative

If you stumble upon an opportunity to take charge and lead a project, take it! There's no better way to prove your expertise than to put yourself in a position where people take your advice and follow your instructions. This is your time to shine and show everyone who you are. By making the most of these opportunities you can make lasting impressions.

8. Be humble and respectful

A true expert doesn't need to brag or purposely try to convince others how great they are. That said, not even mentioning your skills or how successful you are would also be detrimental when you're trying to position yourself as a leading authority in your field. Try to find a balance where people are aware of your knowledge and success but you're not constantly trying to remind them of it.

No matter what you do, you should always respect others and be humble, even if you know more than almost everyone else in your niche. Staying in an authority position is just so much easier when people actually like you, not just tolerate you because of your skills and knowledge. This also shouldn't require much effort from you, so it's a winning strategy in every way. People don't care how much you know unless they know how much you care.

9. Admit when you are wrong

Some leading experts would rather jump from a bridge than admit that they're wrong about something. In the end it can make them look rather foolish. Most industries, online and offline, are constantly changing and evolving, and even a leading authority cannot be expected to always keep up with it all. Sooner or later you'll run into a situation where you're just plain wrong or don't know the answer. Admitting it is always better than being stubborn and acting like you could never be wrong about anything. People will simply respect you more if you admit it!

Actionable Steps To Become An Authority

Becoming an authority, in any field, is not easy. Not only do you need to know more and have better skills than everyone else in your niche, but you also need to market yourself properly and network with others.

Ideas to help you reach authority status

Being a niche authority means gaining the respect of the community, and getting plenty of opportunities to keep evolving and profiting. It's almost like becoming a celebrity of sorts, and some of the perks are definitely similar to those celebrities enjoy (like VIP invitations to events). If you know what steps to take to make the largest impact on your reputation, it will be much easier.

You cannot be an authority figure today without having at least one active social media account. Whether you prefer Twitter, Facebook or Google + it doesn't really matter, as long as you're certain that large parts of your potential audience following uses that platform too. If 99% of the existing authorities in your niche all use one platform you may want to consider sticking to that one as well, as that's obviously what the audience prefers. Don't forget that old-fashioned forums are also great for networking and participating in the community surrounding your niche, so make visiting the largest ones and answering questions a weekly habit.

Write and publish a book

If you want to be treated like an expert in your field, there is arguably no better way than writing a book and having it published. If it sells well then great, if not you can still benefit a lot from it just from the status it gives you to have had a book published. The next time someone questions your authority on the subject, just point to your book and they're likely to change their opinion about you real quick.

If you're lucky enough to pull off a bestseller in your niche you can bet on it to open a lot of doors for you. It may take a few tries to get there, and no doubt there is a lot of work involved, but it is well worth the effort.

It's understandable that writing a whole book might seem daunting, however there are several ways to do it quickly and efficiently through Podcasting and Livestream video or if you love to write just take it one chapter at a time. It doesn't have to be so bad. If you're knowledgeable about the topic but feel like writing isn't really your thing, you can always hire an editor or ghostwriter to write it for you.

There are several ways to use a book. Mike Driggers' very first book (which was only 50 pages) became his business card and instantly put him as an authority in his niche. He only earned $1,600.00 in royalties off the sale of his first book, however it brought him over 300k in revenue that year from different projects. This is very similar to the book you're reading right now. If you would like to learn more about how to easily create and position yourself with a book, then go to www.InstantAuthorityNow.com to get access to 3 FREE in-depth training videos to learn more about this.

Start a podcast

If you feel you have a lot to say about your topic Podcasting is a powerful way to communicate your ideas and messages. By having a Podcast, you bring more exposure, visibility and credibility and shorten the sales cycle passively. You can potentially reach anyone and by doing so your audience gets to know you, like you & trust you as the authority.

There are a few distinct ways that podcasting can provide authority status that aren't as easily done through some of the other avenues. People who start podcasts usually deliver their content in a series, stretched out over a period of time. There are minimal equipment and startup costs if you already own a computer, and so this allows you to use podcasting in a quick and easy way to establish yourself as an authority.

You can interview leaders in your industry or provide education and or information about your product or services. Anyone who has ever dreamed of owning a radio station can be a vocal expert and build social proof and the chance to transmit your ideas far beyond the reach of a radio transmitter.

NOTE: Podcasting is a great way to take the audio recordings and have them transcribed and turned into a book.

Start a Livestream

Similar to podcasting, Livestream allows you to build trust quickly with your audience and instantly positions you as the authority in your niche. Using Platforms like Facebook, Livestream or Periscope allows you to build your very own broadcast channel for your brand and products or services.

Livestream increases transparency with your audience. When you use Facebook, Livestream and Periscope to interact with customers, they appear to be more genuine. They are not anonymous. They are available to answer live questions face to face. Thus, it is believed that Facebook Livestream and apps such as Periscope will become a very integral part of increasing transparency. Using Facebook, Livestream and Periscope is a great way to host interviews.

It's very advantageous for authorities when they interview other industry experts. It makes them look good in the eyes of their niche. Facebook, Livestream and Periscope allows you to host interviews and make them visible to your customers.

Since it's a Livestream, your niche can chat with you and guest speakers. You can also tell customers about the positive feedback that's been received about certain products or services you offer. You can encourage customers to pass along their feedback about the same products or services. This information is beneficial for new customers too.

Start a blog

A lot like Podcasting you should consider starting your own blog. It's a great way to show off your expertise and personality. Fact is, if you want true expert status in your niche, you'll find it very difficult to reach your goal without a blog or some other kind of outlet where people can learn from you and get some insight into who you are and what you know. It will also act as a "business card" of sorts that you can refer people you meet to, so make sure you use a domain name that's easy to remember (usually a .com is preferable over others). Not to mention the opportunities you can find by simply networking and interacting with other bloggers in your niche, so remember to stay active in discussions.

Don't worry if you don't consider yourself much of a writer - as long as you've got something interesting to say, people will listen. If this is a real problem than just create a video blog.

Guest podcasting, bloging and publishing articles

When you're just starting to build up your authority status, chances are you're an unknown nobody in your niche. Even if you have a ton of interesting insights to share on your blog and social networks, you need to draw traffic and eyeballs to them somehow. Guest podcasting, blogging and writing articles for other websites (maybe even magazines) or shows are great for that!

The more listeners, or readers that a blog or website you want to write for has, the harder it will usually be to get your article accepted. Some popular blogs get dozens of guest blogging requests every week, and you need to make sure you stand out.

It definitely helps if you're familiar enough with the podcast/site/magazine to know what kind of content they're looking for so you can tailor your proposal accordingly.

Usually you'll have to start writing for some smaller sites, as the larger and more popular ones will probably want to see other articles you've had published before. You can then refer them to your articles on those smaller sites, and slowly work your way up to the most visited sites in your niche. It may take some time but along the way you will gain more and more recognition, and even direct traffic to your blog from links in the "author bio" section of the articles.

Closely monitor your online reputation

To be an established expert in a field it is imperative you monitor your online reputation. If you on one hand are calling yourself an expert while tons of customers are complaining about your company on Yelp, Google and other online review portals it will be counterproductive. The online community understands that things can happen in a business and that there are a number of highly critical customers. They can also read between the lines by the number of reviews they read. By taking care of your customers and quickly responding to any negative reviews you can maintain the trusts of the online community and in turn maintain your expert status. There is high value when you can put on your website that you have a 5 star rating on Yelp or Google.

Build a social media presence

If you want to become an authority you need some sort of

social media presence, there's simply no way around it. That doesn't mean you have to spend 4 hours every day interacting on social networks, but you should at the very least try to participate once a day.

Which websites to use depends on both your own personal preference as well as the preference of the "community" in general in your niche. In some niches Twitter is king, others seem to prefer Facebook, Pinterest or Google +. If you're uncertain of where to put in most of your efforts, just look at what other authorities in your niche are doing. Are they spending most of their day tweeting, discussing in Facebook groups or something else? Look at what they're doing and try to do it better - just don't straight up copy their approach.

Social networks aren't for everyone, and it seems that most people either enjoy them or hate them. If you're in the latter group you could try to the find the social media outlet that you like the most and focus only on that one. As long as you're doing something and participating somewhere, it's much better than not having a social media presence at all.

Participate on industry forums

If there are any active forums in your niche you should make it one of your main goals to become a well known member of them, perhaps even a moderator. Forums might be considered "old school" by some, but the fact remains that many of them get thousands of visitors every day, and members who take the time to participate can quite easily build up their authority on that particular forum (and in the niche in general).

The same basic rules apply as on social media - try to login and participate in discussions at least once per day. The more the better. Yes, it is definitely time-consuming but the potential rewards are great. When you're an established member of a forum you'll enjoy plenty of perks, such as the ability to draw traffic to your own blog/website. You can also use the forums for announcements, like if you were to write a book and wanted to announce the launch.

In the beginning, though, you should focus on just being helpful and not the slightest bit self-promoting. Just like most other methods, this is a marathon and if you go too fast in the beginning you won't be able to make it to the finish line. Just stick to answering questions and maybe posting a discussion of your own once in a while and you'll see results eventually.

Teach others what you know

Taking on a teaching role is an excellent way to improve your authority. Ever since we were kids we've been told to respect the authority of teachers, and that's something that stays with us. And, by all means, someone who decides to set aside the time and effort required to teach others deserves that respect.

Exactly how you choose to go about it is up to you. You can stick to simply writing tutorials and guides, or you can go "all in" and launch a full course where you teach people everything you know. Either way, to be truly successful with this path you need to be patient and prepare for answering a lot of questions. Teaching can be quite draining, but also very rewarding when you see that your "students" are learning from you.

Network with other experts in your niche

Just associating and networking with other experts in your niche will do much for your reputation and authority. It is also a great way to stay updated with the latest developments in your niche.

Many highly successful experts participate in mastermind groups on a regular basis. Trying to befriend the top authorities in your niche and getting an invite to their mastermind group (if they have one) should be one of your main goals to work towards. Usually people in mastermind groups are very helpful, regularly exchanging knowledge and favors. For example, how much would it help to have one of the largest bloggers in your niche plug your own blog on their social media accounts? It could potentially send thousands of visitors, and have you go from a complete nobody to a recognized authority overnight. That's just how powerful this can be.

As always though, you will probably not be able to jump straight into the elite layer of your niche, but rather start small and work your way up. In many cases starting your own mastermind group and inviting other experts in your niche to it is the way to go when you're just starting out. Just make sure you have something to offer them to make it worth their while.

Speak at events

This is another situation where you'll most likely need to start small, unless you've already built up some reputation and credibility in your niche. Once you've reached a point where people are actually interested in hearing what you have to say, public speaking is an excellent way to cement your status as an authority in your niche.

When you're just starting out, consider focusing on getting a spot at a smaller industry event. You will still need to be able to prove your abilities though, so it helps if you at least have a blog and a small following already. You should also plan in detail what you're going to talk about before reaching out, so you can give them all the details they need and convince them that you'll do a good job.

Host seminars & webinars

While hosting a webinar can easily be done even early on when you're still somewhat unknown, a real-life seminar shouldn't be considered until you've had several successful presentations as a speaker at other events. It's almost like hosting an entire event on your own, relying on your name to attract an audience. It is not something you can do until you've already built up a decent following and become a household name in your niche. Since hosting a real-life seminar can also be a costly affair you'll most likely have to charge for it - another reason why it's not easily done when you're not an established authority already.

Webinars are different though as they require much less effort from the audience, considering they don't have to show up in person. They just have to logon to a website, see what you have to say, and if they don't like it they can just close the browser window. That said, don't think marketing a webinar is super easy either, because it's not. This is where already being an established member of a forum, having a successful blog, or being active on social media can really pay off, as you can market your webinar through all those channels.

Create a community yourself

An alternative to becoming well known in an established community (like a forum) is building one yourself, positioning yourself as the founder, leader and expert. This may be an especially attractive alternative in niches where there aren't a lot of communities already - otherwise you'll find yourself competing in what could be a very competitive space.

You can use any platform you like, ranging from forums to discussions on social media platforms like Facebook and LinkedIn. Whenever possible it's usually better to use a self-hosted option like a forum, as that puts you in complete control over the community. There's no harm in starting by creating a Facebook group and then transitioning to a self-hosted forum later on. In fact that can be a smart thing to do as getting a forum off the ground without an existing audience can be very tough. People simply don't like putting in the effort of participating on what looks like a "dead" forum.

What else?

There are countless other things you can do to improve your authority status. One thing you could do is to sit down and write a list of what you enjoy doing (and what you're good at), then look at every point from an efficiency perspective - how likely is it to contribute to your authority status? Then just focus your efforts on where you think people will notice them the most.

However you choose to do it, be prepared that it will take time and effort before you've built up your community to a decent size, especially if you're in a smaller niche and starting from scratch. Like most things though, it's something you can take one step at a time. It doesn't have to go from zero to super popular in a week!

By the time it is said and done you will find by becoming an established authority in your market it will lead to more success. You will not only get more visitors to you website and business but more of these leads will turn into buyers.

The Authority principle is a powerful tool and should be used as one of the best ways to measure up in front of your past, present, and potential customers. When you demonstrate that you're great at what you do, people will show you the due respect. Use this to position yourself as the expert in your niche.

"Great online Marketing is not a department, a job or a task. Great online Marketing is engaging your potential, past or current customers with information, education, and advising them about your product and services. This makes the customer feel that they made the right decision to buy from you."

CHAPTER 5

DOMINATE YOUR LOCAL MARKET

The big payoff for your business will come when you are dominating the Internet in your local area. This is when the *boom* will really sound and your internet presence takes off.

Local domination means you are the #1 authority on the Internet for your local market. You get that distinction by taking your business from hard to find online to literally being everywhere online. We call this the snowball effect. Effective internet marketing starts off slow like the size of a snowball. But if consistently worked on, over time your internet presence will overtake your competition. It will also outlast the rest of your competition, just like a huge snowball taking on greater layers at every turn.

You'll be in the top 10 of the local search, natural search and pay-per-click campaigns. Your content will show in top results and you'll have more great consumer reviews than any other local business in your market.

Once your business is consistently the most popular one found in any type of online search, and once you're absolutely everywhere your local clients look, potential new clients will quickly recognize you as an authority in your field.

They will want to do business with you, because they will recognize you as the best. And who doesn't want to do business with the best?

Online local domination is simply being the most readily found business of its type in a given local area with great customer reviews. If your business is consistently at the top of the local search results, normal search results, pay per click results and geo-targeted generic results, you have achieved online local domination. If your business is at the top of normal search results not including an indicator of area, it is even better. You have reached even greater domination when you are found in as many keyword searches possible in your local industry.

Front page results are what you need and ultimately what matters most, because 98% of people searching choose from those page 1 results (no matter what search engine they use). In fact, you want to be in the top 3 results for your keywords to get potential clients to your site. If you are not in those results, you are losing out on a lot of business. It is more than worth your while to budget on an online targeted campaign to reach these goals.

Professional online marketers get most businesses to rank on the front-page of Google for local keywords typically within a short period. They do this, because most local keywords have very little competition and are ripe when someone comes around who is knowledgeable.

Local Search Optimization

The key areas to focus on that will help position your business as one of the main players in your Industry include dominating:

1. Local Listings (Google Places / Google Plus)
2. Organic Listings (SEO)
3. Paid Listings (PPC)

Let's take a detailed look at each one.

1. Local Listings

The fastest and easiest way to get noticed and get FREE exposure is through the millions of basic searches for local online businesses. Reportedly 97% of buyers search for local businesses. If you're not visible when those searches are carried out; you're missing out. Check out Google Places for Business. It's a free local platform from Google.

10 facts you never knew about local directories:

- Searches within local directories account for a whopping 10 billion of the searches that are made every month. (GetListed.org).

- Just recently, YouTube overtook Facebook as the largest social networking site, with 165 million active users. At the same time, Facebook dropped to approximately 160 million active users. (CompetePRO.)

- Not too long ago, Google+ Business had 540 million active users. (http://gokyros.com/a-beginners-guide-to-google-my-business/).

- Customers are 31% times more likely to use a business with "excellent" online reviews. (http://www.invespcro.com/blog/the-importance-of-online-customer-reviews-infographic/).

- 88% of users say that they treat positive reviews just as they would by getting a personal recommendation from a friend or family member. That's up from 79%. (http://www.invespcro.com/blog/the-importance-of-online-customer-reviews-infographic/).

- Yelp currently has over 90 million local reviews. (http://expandedramblings.com/index.php/yelp-statistics/).

- Despite these facts, there are still 87% of small businesses that don't use review sites such as Google+ Business or Yelp. (mashable.com).

- When online consumers shop online, 73% of the time they were also searching for a store location. (online-behavior.com).

- Half of the users looking for an online purchase do not start their search with a search engine, but rather through a local directory. (AT&T Small Business Technology Poll 2013 – yola.com).

- 50% of customers who look for a local business through their Smartphone call or visit that business within 24 hours. (https://think.storage.googleapis.com/docs/how-advertisers-can-extend-their-relevance-with-search_research-studies.pdf).

2. Organic Listings

Organic is just as it implies, a natural occurrence whereby pages appear by the dozens. The searches performed by traffickers have a bearing on certain search terms, versus someone placing an ad and having the words popup as an advertisement.

3. Paid Listings

Of course, paid listings are advertisements you've paid to run, for instance on Google, or the many search engines with any significant market share which accepts paid listings; which are ultimately linked to a series of keywords. **To learn more about this topic download our FREE report "PPC & CPA Marketing Excellence"** at http://www.ontargetmarketing.com/cpa/sp

The Power of Search Domination

The overwhelmingly most popular portal to most websites is the search engine. It is estimated 90% of all web traffic comes from search engines. If you don't honor them, you are potentially missing out on a massive stream of traffic.

We keep using search engines plural, but currently Google has such an overwhelming market share it is all we really care about.

When we mention search engines, we are almost certainly talking about the big G. Google recently revealed they are getting over 100 billion searches a month.

When you're looking to become a dominating force in the online arena for your products, services or brand, you can't take the powers of search engines for granted. If you are ranking #1 in Google for your choice of keywords, that might be all you need to drive traffic to your website or offer. Many people make a good living just by using search engines as their traffic streams.

How Do I Honor the Search Engines?

The best time to start worrying about the search engines is BEFORE you even build your website. If you build your site with the search engines in mind you will be off to a great start. Some factors to consider include:

Platform

You want to pick the right platform to build your site. Search engine friendliness is one of the variables when choosing. So, let's just cut to the chase and say *build your site with WordPress*. Google likes it. It's that simple. WordPress is very search engine friendly and WordPress websites and blogs have a proven track record of frequently making it to the top of Google.

Keywords

Keywords are essentially the terms people type into the search engine to find your offer. You must ask yourself, what are the most likely terms buyers are willing to pay for, and what keywords would they use in an online search. Make a list of all the words or groups of words you can. Think of every way someone would attempt to find your product or service.

How Will People Search for You? What types of phrasing will potential customers use when searching for you? Will they look for a person, position, a firm or a solution? Will they use geographic modifiers like city, state or region? Will their level of motivation come through in their search by using specific words?

Specific Person

- "Dentist" or "Dental"

    Geographic modifiers: "Dentist Dallas", "Dentist Dallas Tx"

- Motivation levels:
    "Emergency Dentist Dallas", "24 hour Dentist"

As a critical part of your keyword research, you should employ a keyword research tool. While there are a variety of such tools on the market, Google AdWords is a free one which helps greatly, as it generates keyword ideas for you, as well as synonyms.

Cross reference your keywords with geographic modifiers. This will often help you be as effective as possible getting ranked according to strong keywords. The more precise the keyword, the better conversion rate it will have for sales.

The Google keywords tool will help you build a great list of relevant keywords people are using every single day to find products, or services like yours. Type in Google <u>The Google Keyword Planner</u> or here's a URL to the key word tool.

https://adwords.google.com//**KeywordPlanner**

Once you are there, you can plug in a couple of your keyword terms and Google will give you a whole list of related keyword terms. They will also give you an estimation of how many searches they receive.

You can then download a convenient spreadsheet of all of the keywords. You'll also see if the keyword search you performed showed the keyword results in *low, medium* or *high* searches.

Be sure to keep a running tab of all the keywords you discover. This will give you information to work with for your online content within your website, blog and videos. It will also keep you from having to repeat the keyword search.

Keywords will be used in every aspect of your online marketing. Therefore the research you do in the beginning about your ideal client and how they search will carry over in all your online content. You will use those keywords for:

- Articles
- Blogs

- Website Content
- Search Engine Optimization
- Press releases
- Ads
- Social media
- Videos and audios
- Tags

Even simply adding one or more traffic methods per month to your existing traffic generating strategies will earn significant results. Target a couple more keywords from your keyword list each month. Keywords also play an important role on YouTube titles. Don't forget that Google owns YouTube and looks for key words in the title and a video can make it to the top of searches in some cases. This is powerful because when the video shows up in a Google search you are able to see an eye catching graphic which can encourage more traffic. Google also transcribes the video to ensure the content is in alignment with the title to keep the purity of all keyword searches. So when making the video remember to say as many key words as possible within the video. This keeps Google as the most entrusted and top search engine.

URL:

When starting a new website, one of the first and most important decisions you have to make is choosing a domain name. That choice will impact the website's success in nearly every area, included search engine optimization (SEO) and social media marketing (SMM). Let's examine how a domain name impacts SEO and SMM and then analyze the factors that make a good domain name. If you already have a domain name you can create one or two more domain names and do what is called a redirect to your main domain name. This can help with you SEO. We, however, don't recommend you do more than 2 or 3 redirects because this could actually harm your SEO with search engines because they will consider this spam.

Should I Choose A Keyword Domain?

For years SEOs and search marketers have often purchased domains that contained their targeted keywords in order to increase Click Through Rates (CTRs) and to help gain higher rankings on Google, Yahoo and other search engines. Let's examine this strategy to determine if it is still effective.

Many SEO strategists would purchase Exact Match Domains (EMDs), which are domains that exactly match the keyword phrase they are targeting. For example, if they want to rank for "buy red widgets" the person might purchase BuyRedWidgets.com. EMDs offered three advantages.

1. The presence of the keyword phrase in the domain was itself a ranking factor.
2. The presence of the keyword phrase in the domain encouraged other webmasters to include their websites .
3. The keyword phrase in the anchor text when linking to the website.

However, in light of recent Google updates (especially the "EMD update"), EMDs are no longer as helpful as they once were.

Page Title & Post Titles:

You want to ensure the title of your webpage includes your ideal keywords! The title is usually found in the browser at the very top, above the address bar. If you are on Google, it will say Google at the top of the screen (this is the page title).

It is the first thing Google sees when it looks at your site. It is an important factor in ranking in the search engines. If you use WordPress you can use a plug-in like *All in One SEO Pack* to easily change your page and post titles. Also in WordPress, if you set your Permalinks to **/%postame%/** in your settings, then whatever you name your posts, this is what the web URL will be. For example: www.yoursite.com/your-post-title. This is one way you can get your keywords into your web URL if you have a generic domain name.

Backlinks:

One of the best ways to get your site to rank high in the search engines is to create Backlinks to aim traffic back to your site. Backlinks are simply links elsewhere on the web from other websites leading to your website. If Google finds a lot of these, your site will be more powerful and popular in their eyes. It is to your advantage to create as many Backlinks as possible on high trafficked sites directing visitors back to your site to ensure favor with the search engines.

One major thing to consider is anchor text. Whatever the link actually says which leads to your site is the Anchor Text. You want your keywords to be this text. You don't want your link to say "click here" it is much better if it says "your keyword."

You can find a lot of backlink info online. A couple of popular places used for backlinks are:

- Blog Comments
- Forum Signatures
- Web Directories
- Article Directories
- Social Bookmarking Sites
- Website Profiles
- Other Websites

A backlink guide is an entirely different book, but a Google search on how to get backlinks, should lead you on the right path.

Content:

To us this is the most important step in making your site friendly to the search engines. Google loves fresh content.

In general, fresh content is valued highly by the search engines. Google's main goal is to provide its users with relevant content.

If a website has fresh content, then it usually means the content is more current, therefore relevant. The more relevant the more prominence.

"Every time you are marketing online to a large audience, you have to remember you are only speaking to one person at any given time."

CHAPTER 6

How to Get a Stampede of Targeted Leads to Your Website

First and foremost, traffic is just one part of the equation to get your business booming via online marketing. The other two aspects are having a good converting website and having a solid backend process once your business receives an email, phone call or enquiry from the Internet.

Here's the interesting news though, even if your website is the biggest load of cow dung on the Internet and you have zero conversion strategies on it, if you have 1,000, 10,000 or 100,000 people visiting it each and every month, then you still have a potential goldmine of business. It first comes down to how much visiting traffic you can get to your website. Visitors will almost always result in some sort of business transaction. No online visitors to your website equals - NO online customers. The more online visitors you get to your site will equal MORE online customers. It's just simple!

Hence the purpose of this book is to help business's create a stampede of local target leads to their website and business.

With a stampede of traffic coming to your site on a daily or weekly basis it's easy to make a few changes and PRESTO your phone starts ringing and online orders start flying in.

However, if you have the best converting website in the world and no traffic coming to it, then you are dead in the water. Our point here is: Don't worry too much about getting your website 100% right in the beginning. But, you will definitely need to change it on an ongoing basis to keep your conversion rate high. It is always imperative to be highly focused on driving traffic to your website.

Internet marketing is changing so rapidly your site needs to change with the times, if it doesn't you'll find yourself in a world of trouble real fast and could quickly lose business to your competitors.

Check out the strategies below to discover the best way to get traffic to your site.

What exactly are the best search engine traffic getting strategies?

1. SEO
2. PPC
3. Google Maps

In fact, to dominate Google, the goal is for your site to get found on the front-page of Google as many times and towards the top as much as possible. You can use this section now as your Marketing Roadmap for online success, as we are going to breakdown exactly what you need to do to get the most out of the strategies above.

If we go back to the stats mentioned earlier it'll show you what we mean.

- 98% of searchers choose a business on page 1 of the results gathered from their search.
- 41% of clicks go to the #1 ranked site in a search.
- 12% of clicks go to the #2 ranked site in a search.
- 8.5% of clicks go to the #3 ranked site in a search.

Let's break it down and look at what you can do to tap into the majority of people looking to do business on any given day.

SEO (Search Engine Optimization)

Search engine optimization or SEO is vital to the implementation of your online marketing plan. While this is a part of the 5 one-time things you must do to get your plan started successfully, it must also be monitored and updated. You do this to make sure you keep your local business results and your natural search results ranking near or at the top.

Google Maps (Local Business Listings)

Local business results will impact not only in the traffic to your website, but will also impact the phone at your place of business. Once your business is successfully located at the top of these results, you'll find your phone ringing more often.

It'll ring because your phone number is listed in the local business results.

Submit your business to the three major local business results sites (Google, Yahoo and MSN/Bing). It is also a good idea to use services such as Advice Local or Yext that will place your business in hundreds of online business directories and monitor them monthly for you. This could save you hours and greatly increase your internet exposure. Also, don't forget many mobile apps and MapQuest use online directories to pull from for data in their local searches. Monitor and update listings regularly to secure top spots. It is important to fully develop your business listings with the link to your website, correct address, phone number, logo, up-to-date pictures, services you provide, products you sell, hours of operation, relevant videos and more. Leave nothing undone. Business listings can also be a great source for powerful reviews. Make sure your listings are also search engine optimized.

Three business listing sites you must be on are:
1. Google – the most important one as it owns more than 2/3 of online traffic.
2. Yahoo – It is one of the top 10 sites in the world.
3. MSN/Bing – Growing in importance, but not as prominent as Google and Yahoo.

These local business results each pick up on select keywords and use different location modifiers when ranking listings. However, most listings include address, phone number, directions to a physical address, website, logo, pictures, video and customer reviews.

The ones with the best reviews containing targeted keywords, in addition to location modifiers, will find their way to the top of the search results.

To be listed in the top 10 search results, follow these 7 tips:

1. Optimize every aspect of your listing with strategic keywords.

2. Get reviews from clients. (Video Reviews are more impactful then written reviews).

3. Obtain Backlinks from local online directories. Yext or Advice Local give you the ability to submit your business on their platform and from there they push your information into hundreds of local business directories for you.

4. Strategically choose the areas you want optimized; even establishing different addresses and phone numbers for other areas.

5. Get listed in about 4 to 5 categories related to your business for your business results listing.

6. Place coupons, specials or offers with the listing to increase conversion rates. Make sure the coupon, special or offer has an ending date to create urgency. You can always follow up with a different incentive when the last one expires.

7. Use YouTube videos with your keywords in the title. YouTube is owned by Google and can push your video into internet searches if done correctly. The Title is

important, what is said in the video is very important also because YouTube is transposing your video for accurate relevance. Finish with accurate tags and fill in a great complete keyword rich content in the about part of the video. The great thing about YouTube videos is they can be easily embedded into more directories and your websites. They can also be easily shared into other social media platforms.

Track changes you make. This way, you can keep the listing as relevant as possible. It will also help you monitor what works and what doesn't. Be patient, it sometimes takes a few weeks to see your listing appear. But, when done right it can have a lasting effect.

Organic Listings

Organic listings are also referred to as FREE or natural listings, as they are generated by the search engines themselves and are not paid for. They are typically placed below local searches with the map and paid searches, many people consider them the most valid type of search results.

It is possible to get a variety of listings in the natural results. Anything with relevant content on it, especially if it has been search engine optimized, can be included in natural search results. Search engine rankings can include:

- Your main website
- Social media content
- Articles
- Press releases

- Web 2.0 content
- Landing pages
- Videos
- Social bookmarks
- Directory listings
- Blog posts

Keyword research is vital to the successful ranking of your website, and more important in the natural results of search engines. Therefore this step is not to be overlooked. The relevancy of your content is very important to placement. Other ranking factors which impact where your content shows up in ranking include:

- Content congruency / consistency
- Keywords used in page links
- Keywords used in content
- Links pointing back to your site / content
- Google page rank

In fact, good relevant content and on-page SEO combined with the proper keyword usage, and enough backlinks, will be sure to make it to the top of many categories within a given period of time. Get links to your site from local directories, article marketing/press release syndication, Web 2.0, blogs, social bookmarks, and video marketing. The more quality links you have to your site, the more successful it will be in ranking.

PPC (Pay-Per-Click)

Pay-Per-Click advertising is one area where many people are already investing in online marketing. You may be one of those who recognize the value of such campaigns in finding potential clients. Some studies show that 50% of people arriving at a retailer's site from a paid ad are more likely to buy than those who came from an organic link.

One of the major advantages in PPC campaigns is you can be up and running with traffic coming to your website in as little as one day. With an effective targeted strategy you can be at the top of search engines whereas waiting for natural listings can take awhile because of the competition. We actually recommend you start an effective PPC campaign immediately so you can take advantage of the people searching for your goods or services right away.

Other major benefits, you can easily and accurately measure results and you can achieve incredible ROI (return-on-investment) from well-structured pay-per-click campaigns. Then you can monitor and optimize for future success.

Pay-Per-Click campaigns in some cases can be quite expensive. However, they can be greatly downsized by the effective use of other online marketing strategies. You can easily spend a lot less on your PPC campaign than you have previously (when your business is consistently at the top of search engine results).

However, PPC campaigns are still important tools that can remain as a part of a good online marketing strategy, especially for extremely competitive keyword searches. There is also new technology that allows business owners to run current reports on credit card spending habits with a 25 mile to 3 mile radius of their location. With this information you can run direct PPC advertising ads to these specific customers. This was once only used by large companies such as Target and Wal-Mart but now this information has been made affordable to small business owners.

One last thing to remember about PPC campaigns is, don't underestimate a pay-per-click campaign on Facebook. Facebook has millions of active users and when geo targeted correctly your PPC campaign can drive tons of visitors to your website. You can target consumers in local areas, age range, gender and interests in ways that other search engines cannot. Not every business owner is taking advantage of this powerful option. When done correctly Facebook can generate thousands of leads to your website.

To learn more about this topic download our FREE report "PPC & CPA Marketing Excellence" at http://www.ontargetmarketing.com/cpa/sp

The Right Keyword Research

Keyword research is the *key* (excuse the pun), that makes your PPC campaigns work like never before. If you have your keyword research done correctly, you will have a list of keywords used when people search for something your business can provide, including very specific long-tailed keywords.

These keywords will not only be the ones most commonly used, but also the ones that have the fewest PPC matches for them. This means when someone uses those keywords your ad will appear at the top, not mixed in somewhere with endless others.

Keyword research makes all the difference between hit-n-miss PPC campaigns. Keyword research makes all the difference between a set of keywords that really work, and the ones with a high click-through rate of conversions to sales. Having professional management of your PPC campaigns can mean having huge savings and much greater results.

Geo-Targeting Your Ads

This is one of the most awesome features of running PPC campaigns, as you have the option to target PPC ads to only the people in your area who are searching for a given term.

Using a geo-targeting search from someone in your geographic area for a generic term like "electrician" would reveal your ad; whereas someone in another state or area that you don't serve who searches for "electrician" would not see your ad, (unless you wanted them to).

Using Google Ads and other PPC services, you can choose to have your ads shown only to people living in certain zip codes, cities or regions. By doing so you can bid on very generic terms that previously would not have been a good choice.

This is possible because search engines know where searchers are located. You can choose to target:

- Actual location
- Narrow geography such as city, state, metro area
- IP Address

In addition, you can choose to do PPC campaigns that work with a location qualifier attached to them. Many people will actually choose to include the location qualifier in their search, such as "Miami plumber." By using both the searcher's actual location and where the searcher is looking, you will have the greatest success possible in your Pay-Per-Click campaign.

The advantages to geo-targeting generic terms for your PPC ads are:

- Cheaper click rates
- Fast traffic results
- More targeted traffic
- Lower competition
- Higher conversion to sales

Google also uses smart technology and will direct PPC campaigns toward customers who they are tracking by keywords. Example: When a customer does a search for a local plumber Google recognizes this and will target PPC campaigns of local Plumbers in their area and when the user goes back on the internet they will start to see plumber ads show up in different locations.

The Importance of the Landing Page

A landing page is the page a prospect reaches when they click through your ad, a link in your article's resource box, or a link in a press release, video, business listing, or audio. The best-designed landing pages have a way these visitors can trade their contact information for a special report or some other content that's valuable to them.

The landing page is a very important component in the online marketing strategy for Pay-Per-Click campaigns. It should be relevant to the ad that you have placed and should contain keywords related to the search. You should have a different landing page for each PPC ad you place. Include navigation links to other parts of your site for even better results in Google. If you are going to use your website as your landing page make sure it has all of the key components listed above.

Content Network PPC Campaign

Content network PPC allows you to sell advertising space on your own website and use space on other websites that relate to yours. Content PPC allows you to get your ad in front of people who are not using a search engine but visiting their popular sites.

A large number of websites collaborate in a content network and you get the advantage of the traffic attracted to each of them. Your ad can be much more than a text ad like traditional PPC. You can opt for images and even a video to capture the attention of potential clients. Content network PPC is wide open right now and is an excellent option to explore in your internet marketing plan.

Report Generation, Testing, Tracking

Report generation must be done regularly to stay on top of the performance of your online marketing plan. Through testing and tracking you can effectively and clearly see what is working and *what is not. By doing more of what is working and less of what* isn't working, you'll grow faster at less cost.

This is a very important part of your business and must be done monthly or at least quarterly (unless you are functioning at beyond full capacity). As you are implementing, or even prior to implementing your new marketing strategies, take time to test and track them so you have a baseline to compare against.

Use the following types of data in your analysis of your marketing:

- Rankings
- Links/backlinks
- Traffic sources and volume
- Visitor data
- Visitor actions and behavior

Rankings

You will need to track the main site rankings for the different keywords. This will tell you where each keyword ranks. You can get an idea of the ranking possibilities for the content you put out there using that keyword. You can use rank checker tools to assist you in tracking rankings for keywords. Check those of your competitors also.

Links/Backlinks

When testing your Backlinks for your site, you need to find out where links are coming from. This is simultaneously a test to make sure links are actually working. Track how many Backlinks your site has and how many are recognized by Google.

Do the same for your competitor's, especially those who already have a good degree of online domination. This will give you ideas of where you need to link from. You can access link and backlink tracking tools to facilitate the process.

Traffic Sources and Volume

Traffic sources and the volume of traffic need to be tracked and optimized. This will tell you where your visitor's are coming from and the number of visitors you are getting from each source.

It is important to know if they are direct visitors, referred through natural search engine results, referred from other sites or referred through paid search engine ads. This type of tracking will also reveal the keywords that are working to get visitors to your site. There are traffic tracking tools available for this.

What Are Visitors Doing While On Your Website?

Visitor data should also be tested, tracked and optimized as a regular part of your marketing program. You want to know where they are located, which web browser they use, the type of operating system they use, connection speed and if they are a brand-new unique visitor or a repeat one.

This will help you create the best visitor experience possible for those who come to your site. The same tracking tools that provide traffic data will also help you track visitor data. One of the best free tools for measuring visitor behavior is Google Analytics. All you need to use for this is a free Google account. Once there they will show you how to connect this great tool to your website.

Visitor Actions and Behavior

You will also need to track visitor actions and behavior information. Details like the page of the site the visitor entered on and exited from will divulge the relevant information they were looking for. With such information, you will learn how well your landing pages and other content are working for you. You can also find out how long they stayed on your site; which will help you come up with ways to keep them longer.

Record the links that get the most click-through traffic, so you know what information attracts visitors the most. The most important feature of tracking visitor behavior is to find out the number of people who took action and what they actually did. There are a variety of technologies which allow you to track such information.

By regularly testing and tracking your site by the collecting of important data, you will be equipped to optimize it so you're getting the best results possible. You will know what is working effectively and what needs to be changed.

Discern what the data actually means, so you can change content or make site adjustments if necessary. This will help you improve your business by getting the right people to your site (who will then convert to sales). Here's the link for Google Analytics free download: **www.google.com.au/analytics/**

Other Ways to Drive Traffic to Your Website

Press Releases:

Never underestimate the power of a Press Release. A few well placed keywords throughout a well crafted press release can produce a volume of high traffic. Some use a sales/marketing/press release as a single tool to perform multiple functions. A good writer can spin the content around an entire PPC campaign.

Articles:

As mentioned above, you can write an article about your product or service (or have a creative writer write one for you), then use a group of articles for press releases/marketing and promotions. Simply take the original content, add some facts or stats about your business, add keywords to link to your site, and there you have it.

Social Media:

1. Facebook

There are as many good reasons for your business to participate in the Facebook community as there are people on the web. It's a great way to connect to people searching for what you sell. It's also an easy way for you to converse directly with your customer base.

You have an opportunity to create a community around your product or service. It's easier to generate leads from someone you know or who is in your circle or who knows someone you know. Additionally, you can use your Facebook posts to create and build your SEO Rankings.

A developed Facebook page with thousands of "Likes" allows you to advertise to them for free as much as you like.

How much would it cost you to send out a post card to that many interested customers? A developed Facebook page can save you tons of advertising dollars and create thousands of potential customers on a daily basis. Just remember to use what we call Facebook etiquette. What we mean by this, is don't over post too many sales pitches.

What is most effective on Facebook Business Pages is to give information for free, post reviews, videos and related articles that will drive interests to potential customers without pushing them away. Don't under or over do anything on Facebook. Be wise with how you handle all of the people who liked your business and you will enjoy tons of free advertising. **To learn more about this topic download our FREE report "Facebook Marketing Excellence" at**

http://www.ontargetmarketing.com/facebook/sp

2. Twitter

By the time Twitter came along MySpace was pretty much spammed out. Twitter quickly became the hot new thing everyone was talking about. It suddenly became cool to Tweet. Rest assured those small Tweets you perform within seconds grow big nest eggs. It's one of the fastest ways to grow your brand presence. **To learn more about this topic download our FREE report "Twitter Marketing Excellence" at http://www.ontargetmarketing.com/twitter/sp**

3. YouTube

Send people to YouTube to watch your videos and don't forget to ask them to subscribe to your channel. Customers who are subscribed to your YouTube channel will be given an update whenever you post a new video. Use Facebook as your gateway to connect with people, and then send them to YouTube or push your YouTube videos back into your Facebook page. Because of the importance of Facebook, it's particularly essential to incorporate content from all social media like YouTube to extend your reach across the web. Create as many YouTube videos as possible. Each individual video can show up on search engines when keywords are done correctly. When they show up a picture is visible on search engines increasing exposure. **To learn more about this topic download our FREE report "Youtube Marketing Excellence" at**

http://www.ontargetmarketing.com/youtube/sp

You can never under estimate the power of videos. Creating videos with information in your area of expertise, advertisement and customer reviews are very impactful.

4. SlideShare

If you're not familiar with SlideShare, it's quickly becoming a busy slide hosting service. You can upload files privately or publicly using Power Point, PDF, etc.

5. Pinterest

If you're unfamiliar with Pinterest, then get to the website and create an account. Why is this important to you? Because it is now the most effective means of driving traffic (and sales) to your website and it's a more powerful tool for social networking than Facebook and Twitter. **To learn more about this topic download our FREE report "Pinterest Marketing Excellence" at http://www.ontargetmarketing.com/pinterest/sp**

6. LinkedIn

LinkedIn is the world's largest professional network with nearly 200 million members at the time of writing this and rapidly growing. LinkedIn connects you to your trusted contacts and helps you exchange knowledge, ideas, and opportunities with a broader network of professionals.

LinkedIn gives you the ability to create a professional profile that helps establish your credibility in the marketplace. It also enables you to find experts and ideas to help resolve business challenges with a specialized search feature that lets you explore their network of professionals by name, title, company and location.

Also, other business owner's look to network with other business owners thru LinkedIn and you could create partnerships with companies that could bring you thousands of dollars. **To learn more about this topic download our FREE report "LinkedIn Marketing Excellence" at http://www.ontargetmarketing.com/linkedin/sp**

7. Instagram

Instagram is an online mobile photo-sharing, video-sharing and social networking service that enables you to take pictures and videos and share them on a variety of social networking platforms, such as Facebook, Twitter, Tumblr and Flickr. Instagram users can view their news feed and browse other users' profiles and in today's world, marketing is all about sharing the things that are happening right now with your business or product offerings.

To learn more about this topic download our FREE report "Instagram Marketing Excellence" at

http://www.ontargetmarketing.com/instagram/sp

8. Periscope

For many businesses this new tool from Twitter is an interactive video streaming/ broadcasting service app that makes it easy to broadcast messages or have video conversations through your iPhone or Android. You can basically start your own broadcasting station for your business. You can make your messages public or private and you can go live "on the go" anytime and anywhere. This is powerful tool for creating brand awareness. **To learn more about this topic download our FREE report "Periscope Marketing Excellence" at** http://www.ontargetmarketing.com/periscope/sp

Additional Traffic Strategies

By using a wide variety of traffic strategies, you will have the best chance of being able to attract the maximum number of potential clients to your website. Apart from the techniques already mentioned, there are other ones that will help you drive traffic to your site.

Some of them are completely free, while others involve a varying amount of investment (depending on the quality of equipment you want to use to create them). **To learn more about this topic download our FREE report "Affiliate Marketing Excellence"**

at http://www.ontargetmarketing.com/affiliate/sp

Classified Ads

By placing carefully created online classified ads you can easily drive traffic to your website. Many of these websites are free of charge, like craigslist.org and backpage.com. You can choose to put an ad in the sections which best fit the services or products your company provides.

You can even put links directly back to your website in many of these ads. The sheer volume of traffic on such sites will help people find you and your website more readily, as there are numerous people who use such sites as their *go-to* resource for many things.

To get the maximum amount of use from your classified ads, create links to your ad using social bookmarking sites and other social networking sites. This will create additional backlinks to your ad and help it get ranked in the search engines.

Any content that gets ranked in the search engines is excellent for your online marketing.

Make sure the ads you place on classified ad sites are search engine friendly (like all of your online content). Use keywords correctly, without stuffing them into the ad, this will maximize your search engine result ranking.

Such ads need to be placed weekly or monthly to stay current in the search engines. Vary the content though and add seasonal specials, if appropriate.

Some of the best classified ads include:

- Craigslist.org
- Backpage.com
- Topics.com/classifieds/city
- Olx.com
- Oodle.com
- Kijiji.com
- Usefreeads.com

Local Online Discussion Forums

Make sure you are active in local online discussion forums. This will help you reach even more potential new clients. Many times people seek out forums in an attempt to solve a problem they are facing. By being present and taking part in discussions, you can offer your services to solve appropriate issues.

In addition, you will be connecting with potential customers who speak openly about what they can't find or what is not being offered. This is great to do, because you're researching to fine-tune your offerings. This will ensure you are actually meeting the needs of those you want to buy from you.

You can find such local forums by doing a simple online search on them. Most require you to create a free account and profile. Your profile should include information on your business and include a link to your site.

Some tips for optimal use of local online discussion forums as a part of your marketing strategy include:

- Start or contribute to conversations in a relevant way.
- Pay close attention to the forum rules.
- Realize blatant advertising is a no, no.
- Use an anchor text keyword in your signature.
- Use "how to" articles as good posting content for the forums.

Post weekly or monthly on local online discussion forums to take advantage of the benefits, such as multiple backlinks generated from each post.

CHAPTER 7

WHAT MAKES A HIGH CONVERTING WEBSITE?

Very few people talk about this, but here is what we call the *Business is Booming* equation we use to ensure success with any business wishing to market online and grow their brand presence.

Website + Traffic + Conversions = Success

With this in mind let's look at part 3 of the *Business is Booming* equation; which is how to effectively convert visitors that come to your site to phone calls, email enquiries, opt-ins (if you are list building), or to direct sales (if you have an e-commerce site).

First you will need to begin by analyzing your current site. Review the following:

- The look and feel of the site.
- Is the site optimized for visitors?

- Does your site clearly define what you do?
- Does it show on the top where you are located?
- Can customers easily contact you.
- Does your site have a call to action.
- Does your site funnel visitors to customers?
- Is the site optimized for search engines?
- Does the site work for multiple browsers?
- Is your site linked into your Social Media?
- Does your site have a captivating video?
- Does your site clearly define within seconds what your company does?
- Is your site filled with powerful customer video and written reviews?
- Does your site have captivating easy to look at colors and pictures?
- Is your site mobile and tablet friendly?

35 Essential Components of a High Converting Website:

In most cases, websites are lacking in some of these areas. In order to make your website appealing to human visitors and search engines, and be effective in its purposes, you will need to go through and make sure the following things are in place. If they are not in place you need to include them for the best results possible.

Use this list as a checklist against your website (or any site you may be planning to develop), either now or in the future. You'll be guaranteed to maximize your sites conversion potential.

1) Ease of Navigation:

- Make sure the site is easy to use and straight forward.

2) Most Important Info above the fold:

- Make sure all the important information is visible when a visitor first arrives at the home page. A good number of people will not scroll down to find the important information. It has been proven that websites convert more visitors to customers when the top of your homepage clearly defines what you do, where you are located and how to contact you.

3) Lead Visitors through the Site:

- Make sure you are taking visitors exactly where you want them to go on your site.

- The sales funnel effect on your site should include a free offer. This is your "magnet offer" to get their contact information. A name, phone number and email address.

- The second part of the funnel is what can be called a tripwire. A tripwire is typically a low selling item to just get them to start doing business with you. This can be from $1.00 to $99.00.

- The Third part of the funnel would be your core offer. This can vary from business to business.
- After they buy your core offer you move your customers into up-sales.
- The final part of the sales funnel is to graduate a customer to buy a big ticket item from your company. If you attempt to move a customer to fast they may not buy anything from you.

4) Multiple Calls to Action:

- Call Now! Buy Now!
- You get 100% of what you ask and don't ask for! Your site is not there to just give information about what you do. Your website is there to convert visitors into buying customers. Calls to action direct visitors into making this happen. Give them a good reason to call you or buy from you ***Right Now***!

5) Subscription Box:

- Make it easier for visitors to subscribe to your site by having subscription boxes. Another fantastic way to pull traffic is to invite blog readers (if you have one), to your blog and RSS feeds. (**R**ich **S**ite **S**ummary; originally RDF Site Summary; often called Really Simple Syndication. Uses a family of standard web feed formats to publish frequently updated information: blog entries, news headlines, audio and video.). You'll boost exposure and boost traffic.

6) Videos on the Site:

- It's not enough in the twenty-first century to have a site. You must think about including a video presentation as a key feature of your site. You can attempt to produce the video however; many prefer to hire a professional to produce a video for their site to promote their products or services. Statistics show that visitors will stay on a site longer when there is video present. **To learn more about this topic download our FREE report "Video Marketing Excellence" at http://www.ontargetmarketing.com/video/sp**

7) Phone Number on Top Right:

- Don't hide your phone number at the bottom of the front page, put it at the top of every page so potential customers can easily call you.

8) Mobile Browsers:

- Back to the 21st Century note above. To coin a phrase, *Time is Money*, and you lose traffic every day you do not have a website with mobile browsing capabilities. People around the globe use their Smartphone to key in products and services. Oftentimes, they choose to buy when they locate what they need. Don't miss out on revenue by not having mobile friendly browsing website.

9) Pages Should Include:
- Home Page
- Products Page
- Service Page
- Customer Reviews
- About
- Contact Form

10) Address Details:
- Always add to the Footer & Contact Page

11) Email Form:
- A lead capture system is simply an opt-in box offering more information, an E-Newsletter subscription, a free report or some other freebie in exchange for simple contact information.
- Typically the information requested is just a name and e-mail address, but some systems ask for a mailing address and, or a phone number. Try to

refrain from requesting too much information. Some people will not give out their personal information when first coming to your site.

12) Call to Action on Every Page:

- At the top of the page
- At the bottom of page
- In the middle of the page

13) Good Content:

- Ensure all text on your website is search engine optimized with strategic use of keywords and avoid duplicate content.

14) Make Unique Selling Propositions Clear:

- Let visitors know what is unique about the way you do business. This will help you stand out from the crowd.

15) Personal Branding:

- Photos of you and your staff
- Branded vehicles
- Audio and video messages
- Professional Logo
- Links to any social networking sites, Facebook, Twitter or other.

16) Correct Use of Images and Pictures:

- This includes proper sizing of pictures as well as using captions to explain what the pictures and images represent. A picture is worth a thousand words, so make them count.

17) Non-Distracting Design:

- This goes for a background that is too distracting as well as crazy fonts, colors, italics and underlines.

18) Trust Factors Like:

- Better Business Bureau
- Association Logos
- Editorials
- Awards
- Seal of Approval from Trusted Brands

19) Credit Card Logos:

- Visa, MasterCard, and American Express

20) Multiple Ways to Contact Your Company:

- Phone number on the top, side and bottom
- Address should be at the top and bottom

21) References/Customer Reviews:

- Video reviews are more powerful than just written reviews. Try to get as many reviews as you can. Make sure to place reviews on your front page and in key locations on your website.

22) Relevancy:

- Search engines love websites that show relevancy. This is done by picking broad and then drilling down in themes. Always optimize one keyword per page instead of multiple keywords per page.

23) Video from the Owner(s):

- Hearing directly from the owner can help build trust with all of your customers.

24) Blog + Frequency of Posts:

- Recent and relevant information lets your customers know you are up to speed with changes in your industry.

25) Avoid Flash, Frames and Music:

- These items can slow your website down and before the customer even sees your site they may opt to move on to another site if it takes too long to load or is annoying.
- Page speed makes a huge difference if people

will stay on your site or not. Web pages should load within 3 seconds. Any slower and visitors may abandon your site, reducing conversions and sales.

26) All Links Working:

- Don't frustrate visitors or the search engines with broken links. Test and make sure everything is working correctly on your site.

27) RSS Feeds Installed:

- RSS allows customers to quickly receive updates from your website.
- Subscribers receive new content automatically in their feed reader.

28) Facebook:

- Harnessing the power of Facebook cannot be underestimated. When strategized correctly Facebook can drive thousands of visitors to your website. Make sure you place the logo and link to Facebook on your website.

29) Twitter:

- Twitter is not only a source for quickly communicating with your customers but a great tool for targeting potential customers.

30) Pinterest:

- Keep your focus on your brand and don't overpower with pictures and content focusing on you alone. Your goal should be to stick out ahead of the crowd.

31) Optimization for Keywords:

- Using good keywords is huge for search engines and you must take some time to do keyword's research before you can determine if keywords are optimized properly.

32) The Title, Captions, Alt Text & Description Fields:

- These are the most ignored and underutilized features that can improve your content and bring more people to your site.

33) Nice Easy To Read Fonts:

- Arial
- Georgia
- Times Roman
- Verdana
- Use common fonts found on all computers, smart phones and tablets.

34) No Underline, No Italics:

- If you feel the urge to underline or italicize use **BOLD** lettering instead. This creates an easy to read online platform.

35) Centered Layout:

- Layout that has dark text on a light background statistically converts better than reverse text.

CHAPTER 8

STRATEGIC ONLINE SALES FUNNELS - BUILDING THE PERFECT SALES FUNNEL

What is a sales funnel? The sales funnel is a marketing process where you take prospects through a number of steps to get them familiar with you and your products so they feel comfortable enough to purchase from you. The funnel is a metaphor that's used to convey the various stages of the selling process. Sales funnels can be used with any type of business.

A sales funnel is a model that's used to organize the whole process of selling, starting with lead generation to sales. The main advantage of using this model is that it forces you to focus on qualifying your prospects - identifying who is most likely to actually buy from you. That way, you're not just blindly advertising and trying to sell to people. Instead, you're targeting your ideal customer, and not wasting undue resources on trying to sell to people who aren't really interested. The idea is that as someone goes through the sales funnel they become more and more engaged and spend more and more money. Quite simply, a sales funnel is a series of offers that are presented to the customer and tend to increase in both value and price. In a nutshell, a sales funnel is a marketing system that leads someone through a systematic process with the goal of purchasing your product or service.

The idea behind it is to turn a lead into a prospect, then a prospect into a customer, who finally becomes a repeat customer buying over and over again.

What are leads, prospects and customers?

1. Leads – are anyone who is aware of your business or someone you have decided to 'market' for a sale. Leads vary greatly from one another and they can be further segregated into what's known as 'qualified leads' or 'warm leads'. These are groups of people who fit a set criteria. For example, if you're selling golf products, a qualified lead is someone who plays golf rather than a casual sports fan who is not too enthusiastic about the sport.

2. Prospect – is someone who has either a contact with your business or is interested in what you offer as they have signed up to your newsletter or shown interest. Prospects are interchangeable with qualified leads.

3. Customers – well we don't need to explain what a customer is too much we hope. This group can be further separated by customers who have made a single purchase to customers who are repeat buyers.

How Do Sales Funnels Work

At the 'front-end' of the funnel is a free product to capture people's interest.

In order to grab the free product people have to sign-up and hand over their email address - and in turn they are added to a database of prospects. After the person is added to the list, they can then be sent other related offers that they might be interested in. Immediately after signing up for the free product the prospect will typically be presented with a low priced offer called an 'up-sell' or 'one time offer'.

Here they're moving into the 'back-end' of the funnel. If they buy this low priced offer then they will then be offered another related product at a higher price. If the person buys the higher product they are then offered another product at an even higher price... and so on.

As the price of the products increases, so does the value being offered. For example, the free and low-priced up-sell product might be a short 30 to 40 page report or eBook. By the 3rd or 4th up-sell they might then be offered a personal coaching program charged at $497 a month. The idea is that as people go through the sales funnel they become more and more engaged and spend more and more money.

Why do I need sales funnels in my online business?

If you've ever taken the time to study psychology and consumer behavior, then you know the people who've shown an interest in your product are the ones who are most likely to purchase from you again. They already bought from you once thus proving they believe in what you have to offer. If you spend the majority of your time and energy marketing to this group of people, then you will get higher conversion rates, because you are making the most of your time and resources.

A sales funnel will increase your sales revenue

When you think about it, it's absolutely crazy not to offer people multiple products to buy. Let's say you've got a report you're selling for $20. If you leave it at that and get 500 sales, then you'll make $10,000. A nice result - but don't you think that some of those people would be interested in another related product priced at $47? And, don't you think some of those people would be interested in buying another product at $497?

Of course many of those people WON'T be interested - but a proportion WILL. So, if you don't have a sales funnel then you're going to miss out on a LOT of sales.

It's really that simple!

Using a sales funnel will increase your conversion rate

While you move down the sales funnel, you'll notice the number of people in each phase decreasing. However, the people who are still in the sales funnel are likely to buy your product or service.

The nature of the sales funnel filters out the non-perspective buyers while building up the number of targeted prospects. As the funnel narrows, the end result becomes more targeted. As such, you can create a fertile environment with highly targeted customers, where you can focus your marketing efforts. By focusing your efforts on these people, you can appeal to their wants and needs, because they already have a higher chance of converting.

A sales funnel can help predict your sales volume

With a sales funnel, you can use each marketing phase to quantify the number of perspective customers, and then take that data to predict the percentage who will become actual customers.

For example, if Jane monitors her website traffic for six months and finds that she gets 5,000 visitors to her website every month, and out of those visitors, 40% of them sign up for her free product/email newsletter, that's roughly 2,000 new subscribers per month. Of those 2,000 new subscribers per week, 5% of them end up becoming paid subscribers or purchasing one or more of her products.

With this information, Jane can then determine based on the number of people in each stage of the funnel, how many sales she can expect to make.

A sales funnel can help identify marketing obstacles and deficiencies

Keeping a close eye on your traffic and statistics from your analytics program will help you keep track of what's going on in each stage of the marketing process. You can watch for trends in each stage. As you notice these trends, you can pinpoint issues where you have room for improvement.

Using this insight, you can either make adjustments to your plan to improve it, or you can learn where you need to focus more of your efforts to improve your results. If necessary, you can change your strategy, or concentrate on a particular strategy to see what it does.

If Jane notices a change in response to calls to action during certain months, she can adjust the number of emails she sends to her list, either up or down accordingly.

Now, let's take a look at the process you can follow to setup your own sales funnel and put it to work for you.

Setting up your first sales funnel

When you're setting up a sales funnel for the first time it can be overwhelming to decipher all the information out there. In this section, we're breaking down the basics so they're not only easier to understand, but they are also easier for you to implement.

Squeeze pages

A squeeze page may also be called an opt-in page, or a landing page. The one and only purpose of this page is to turn your website visitors into subscribers. Subscribers are the ones who make up your email list, which you use for the purpose of tracking traffic and conversion rates. The email list exists also so you can send emails without being considered "spam."

So, where does the name "squeeze" page come from? Simply put, it "squeezes" your reader until he or she feels there is no other choice than to release his or her name and email address to you. Readers do this because they are interested in what you have to offer, or that free gift you're giving away is just too irresistible. Many people won't subscribe to other lists, but they're willing to subscribe to yours because of what you have to offer them.

When it comes to building an effective squeeze page, certain things must be done, while other things must be avoided.

What you must do

- Research and learn about your target audience, down to small details. Start with a general subject, then find your niche, then find your sub-niche. The more targeted you are, the higher chance of your conversion rate. For instance, let's say you want to break into the pet care niche. Pet care is your general subject, where dogs could be a niche, and Doberman Pinschers could be your sub-niche.

- Use bullet points to list your main selling points. These are easy to scan, which is a plus for both you and your readers.

- Include a call to action. Your readers are likely to see the box where they need to fill in their name and email address—they like easy— and easy means spelling out exactly what you want them to do next.

- Add a relevant video. Videos have been proven to increase conversions by as much as 80%.

- Display real testimonials from previous customers to improve authenticity.

- Offer a free trial or a guarantee to provide the customer with a safeguard when buying.

What you must avoid

- Putting links to anything other than your email list subscription form on your squeeze page. The goal here is to keep them on this page until they give up their valuable contact information. This page does not exist to sell your product—this comes later in the sales funnel. This page is only there to collect subscriber information, and get people interested in what you have to offer.

- Making the squeeze page too long. Do not include more detail than you need to get the job done—getting the reader to sign up. A one page sign up box will work far better than a five page long sales letter.

- Losing sight of the fact that your most important job is to make your readers want more. When your readers want more, they'll come to you for it. Leaving the reader wanting more is the big secret of seeing success with your sales pages.

Entry points

An "entry point" is any external website or vehicle that leads visitors to your squeeze page. You can use any number of techniques to increase the number of entry points you have out there. The more entry points, the more likelihood people will come to your offer.

Here are some examples of valid entry points:

- Solo ads.

- Links in press releases or newspaper articles.

- Articles posted in article directories with a link to your site in the resource box.

- Blog posts written with SEO in mind to draw in organic search engine traffic.

- Pay-per-click advertising campaigns with search engines and/or social media websites.

- Email marketing – Your list is full of people who are interested in what you're selling, create a well crafted email with a link leading them to your landing page.

- Social media – followers who have subscribed to your social media accounts are once again interested in your business, and are strong leads. They can certainly be turned into customers using the right tactics.

An often forgotten, yet critically important "entry point" is word-of-mouth. On the Internet, this is known as "buzz." Generating buzz about your product or service on the Internet is one of the best and fastest ways to increase your reach, and your conversion rates.

Here are some examples of ways to generate buzz:

1. Product reviews

2. Social Media websites such as: Twitter, Facebook, Instagram, and Pinterest
3. Forum posts

Expert recommendation is a new way to leverage the word-of-mouth entry point. When an authority source within a niche tells you about a superior product, the social proof they offer carries a lot of weight. However, it is important to remember: if you are the one doing the recommending, then you need to make sure you deliver on your promise.

Don't recommend things you haven't used, or wouldn't use. You'll lose your creditability and authority in no time!

Freebies

This is the traditional and among the most common way to entice people to opt-in to your list. By offering a freebie that promises to provide them with information they've been desperately searching for, on a subject they are passionate about (ideally your niche or sub-niche) you'll be providing an irresistible offer, and increase your subscriber opt-in rate.

Here are a few rules to follow when building your freebie. Follow them, and most of your battle is won!

- Keep the freebie short, and packed with value.

- Let readers know you have more detailed information.

- Provide readers with at least one, if not more, pieces of valuable information.

- Fill in a gap that no one else has filled.

- Solve a problem that everyone's busy talking about, but no one else is solving.

- Now, you can't just give your freebie away and leave it at that, or you'll never make a sale. You must make it clear to your reader that even though you've solved one problem or addressed one point, the paid product or service you have to offer covers the subject in more detail. Basically, you're using the freebie to lead them to the next stage in the sales funnel. You are now drawing them closer to becoming a paid customer.

- Traditionally, a "special report" much like a shorter version of this eBook is offered, but you don't have to limit yourself to just that.

Here are 5 few other options you may want to consider:

1. Five to seven-day audio course (free or cheap to produce with a microphone and a sound program such as Audacity).

2. Five to seven-day email course (free or inexpensive to produce, depending on whether you write it yourself, or hire someone to write it for you).

3. Video (free or inexpensive to produce with the right equipment and software).

4. Webinar.

5. Newsletter.

You're really only limited to whatever your imagination comes up with, however, you should keep these two golden rules in mind as you develop your free product:

1. The purpose of your freebie is to market to your ideal customer, and get them to sign up to your list. You don't want anyone else on your list!

2. Your freebie needs to be the logical first step of what you have to offer. It should start with low end and move to high end, running parallel with your marketing plan.

Following up on leads with an auto-responder

A landing page combined with a well thought-out lead generating campaign can get you hundreds or thousands of leads. With so many leads it's impractical to email each one individually. This is where we reveal our secret weapon…

The Auto-Responder

An auto-responder is a way of sending preset emails to your leads over a period of time. These emails are not sent to all of your list, but rather to individuals who meet certain requirements. For example, people who have given you their email via your landing page can be segregated to receive preset emails. Auto-responder strategies vary depending on your goals. A typical auto-responder setup may look like this:

Email 1 (Day 1) – Thank them for showing interest in your product or service.

Email 2 (Day 3) – Offer them free useful content in the way of blog articles, eBooks or other digital products.

Email 3 (Day 5) – The Hard Sell. Send them the sales pitch to your product or service with a link to buy at the bottom.

Email 4 (Day 7) – If successful, you can then follow up with an 'up-sell' that involves selling more of your products or services. If they didn't buy, you can put them on another auto-responder using similar methods as above to try again.

This is just a basic example of how you can utilize an auto-responder to follow up on prospects and turn them into customers. Depending on your specific goal, auto-responder setups can be really advanced involving a number of steps.

There are several reliable platforms to choose when you're looking to create a newsletter or auto-responder strategy. We personally recommend Mailchimp or Aweber for your email marketing solutions.

Low-price offers

There's no Internet marketing rule book that says you have to follow the traditional line of thought in where you place your offers throughout your sales funnel. However, low priced offers are a solid marketing tactic that many use to get the job done.

However, if there is a bigger demand for your product you

may easily be able to get a higher price for it. At the same time it is important to remember your target audience's actual budget. If it's too expensive for them, they won't buy it!

When you create your first low priced offer, you can present it as a limited time special. Typically, there's a special offers section for forum members. Before you post your offer though, make sure you've become actively involved in the forum, providing helpful information to the community. Also, make sure you're following the forum's rules for special offers. Just popping in to post a special offer without regard to the community itself means no one will listen to you.

Posting your special offer in a forum helps you in two ways:

1. You'll get feedback, and hopefully, testimonials from people in your target audience, so you can adjust anything that may need to be adjusted, and you can correct any mistakes they may point out to you.

2. You'll get the word-of-mouth, along with the potential for joint venture partnerships, or affiliates who will market your product or service along side you.

Up-Sells

Whether you realize it or not, you're already familiar with up-sells. It's an additional offer at a higher price, included in the product you just sold, or are about to sell.

A simple real life example: If you visit a fast food restaurant, and the cashier asks, "Would you like fries with that?" When you say yes, you've just been up-sold. This increases the amount of money you've spent at the establishment, and in that purchase.

As an Internet marketer, you can do the same thing to catch the customer when they check out, by offering a relevant up-sell.

New marketers often make the mistake of attempting to sell an unrelated product. Customers do not take the offer as the next logical step, and therefore are not interested in whatever it may be.

In our example, burgers and fries often go hand in hand. They logically go together, and if you're not already ordering a combo meal with fries and a drink, the cashier is going to try to get you to. You'll save money compared to buying them all individually, so you feel good, but either way, the restaurant gets more out of your pocket than if you would have just bought the burger.

On the other hand, if the restaurant cashier asked you if you wanted a burrito with your burger…you'd wonder why, and would have said no.

You can introduce your up-sells in other places besides your check out page, too.

Some options include:

- The download page
- The "Thank you" page
- In selected emails to your subscribers

- With a membership site, you can offer a lifetime membership, or upgrades that come with additional resources or more privileges

As you're planning a campaign or writing a product, think about up-sells, and how you will work them into all the parts of your sales funnel...especially as you build your first sales funnel.

Down-Sells

Not all your customers are going to bite on the up-sell offer, even if it is a good one. Maybe they don't need the additional product, or they don't have the budget for the additional cost. Depending on where your up-sell is, you may lose them as customers, but you don't have to! The down-sell swoops in and offers them a cheaper alternative, while still providing something deeply and closely connected to the product you're trying to sell.

Typically, you can re-purpose your original product into a "stripped down" version of the main product. For example, if the product you're offering includes a monthly CD and software package, with PDF reports, and audio files… you can send the PDF reports and the audio files, at a lesser price— so people still get something meaningful to them.

This way you're taking a less expensive version of your product for people who cannot afford the higher priced version of your product—so you don't risk alienating any part of your audience.

Regardless, your down sell needs to be a quality product. Otherwise, you're scamming customers, and you won't get far with that. The last thing you want people to feel is that they didn't get the value they expected—they should be valuable and worthy to you, regardless of how much money they are willing to spend with you.

After the customer purchases your down sell, they'll most likely want to learn more. They will purchase the original product when they're able to do so. If you're really good, they'll buy your up-sell when presented with the opportunity again, to get even more!

Put your down sell in a place the user would see only after he or she declines the product or the up-sell.

Cross-Sells

The cross sell is when you recommend additional products that either enhance or compliment yours. You add these in the same places you include your up-sell offers.

You can use another one of your products, or a product you're an affiliate for as your cross sell. The key here is, you need to be cross selling products that offer a high perceived value—so that your customer sees your offer as genuinely helpful, rather than an attempt to get even more money from them.

When utilized correctly, cross sells will not only increase your profits, but will create a deeper emotional attachment to you. This will position you as a person who truly cares and is looking out for your customers.

Recurring income products and services

This is the jackpot. This is what all Internet marketers are striving for, as real profit lies here. You don't have to sell over and over. These people know you, and are interested in what you have to offer. They're the ones who are always near the bottom of the funnel and buy the most from you. When you pitch an offer they will be right there ready to buy over and over again.

Creating recurring income & repeat customers

- Build Trust with Your Customers: Show your customers they can trust you by using your free and lower priced items.

- Over-deliver: No, we don't mean bombard your new customers with random freebie bonuses. We mean going the extra mile to be helpful. For example, when you offer a free report on how to build squeeze pages… offer an unannounced bonus of four awesome squeeze page designs.

- Know yourself…Pace Your Offerings: Recurring income happens at the right moment. If you can provide compelling proof of your expertise, it could be nearly instantaneous.

- Be Consistent: Plan your offers and how they will progress. You do not want to disappear for months at a time, and you don't want to flood your subscribers email box. If you disappear, you'll likely get deleted or unsubscribed, when you come back, because people won't remember who you are or why the subscribed in the first place.

- Teach Your Customers You are the Go-To Guy/Gal for What they Need: Use the other methods that you use to build links and credibility: such as answering questions on niche forums, testimonials, etc. This is where you position yourself as an industry expert.

With all this out of the way, it's now time to invite your customers to grab offers that will help you build a recurring income.

Some options include:

- Long term courses.
- Group coaching.
- One-on-one coaching.
- Paid membership websites.
- Upgraded membership levels on the membership websites (elite, platinum, diamond, etc..).
- Monthly reports, audio, or video "clubs".

Conclusion

By now, you should have a pretty good idea of what you want your sales funnel to look like, and how you're going to fill it in with offers. You may also have a fairly good idea of how many products you want to produce, as well as the timeline you want to follow to get maximum exposure and profits.

Your sales funnel will:

- Increase your sales!
- Help narrow down your visitors into more targeted consumers.

- Help you focus your marketing efforts to increase your conversion rates and profits.
- Help you identify holes in your marketing plans and strategies.
- Help you predict your sales volume.

Though you will have a larger number of people at the top, and a smaller number of people at the bottom, and it seems like you would really want it the other way around, the targeted customer is really what you're after.

The sales funnel works so you can spend most of your time and marketing budget marketing to the people who are already more likely to buy from you. Though you'll have less people near the bottom of the funnel, the fact that those people are more likely to buy from you than the people at the top makes them that much more valuable to you. You'll get more BANG for your buck, in a sense.

When you build a sales funnel, recognize that not all your customers will start at the top. Your brand new customers may start at the top, but some customers may start in the middle, even though they've not purchased from you, because they have a referral from one of your other customers.

Your existing customer base is usually toward the bottom, because they are much more likely to buy from you again, than someone who is brand new to you.

The key to success in your business is knowing how your sales funnel works. Also, make it parallel to your marketing plan, and have customers in all stages of your sales funnel. This way, when customers buy from you, you can move more people down to the bottom, and keep the customers in reserve for repeat buys and recurring income.

Build your sales funnel by focusing on providing your customers with quality freebies and products that will serve a need or solve a problem they cannot get solved anywhere else.

Fill your website with quality content that will help bring visitors in naturally to you through organic search. Spread the news of your website and offers through PPC campaigns, guest posting, forum posts, getting testimonials and product reviews from people in your target audience, etc.

Focus on quality customer service. Go above and beyond, and you'll earn the respect of your customers. Your reputation, positive or negative, will spread. This can make or break your business, so focus on making it positive and you'll be that much closer to success.

Much of your business, with the proper planning and work beforehand, can be executed on autopilot. You can create the products, sales pages, and auto responders, so that everything is taken care of without intervention from you. This is a great way to build passive income. However, you'll have to keep an eye on things, so you can make sure that you don't disappear, and you're responding to your customers needs. You may have to pop in with a special offer from time to time to stay current. Even on autopilot with passive income, you should still be actively working toward your next promotion or product.

CHAPTER 9

Mobile Marketing – How To Generate More Leads & Sales

When consumers today need or want something, they reflexively reach for their phones. They want the right answer, right away. In this mobile age, instead of a few "moments of truth" or a Zero Moment of Truth, consumers experience countless micro-moments throughout the day while exploring interests, solving problems, searching for products, and making decisions. These micro-moments are the new battleground for hearts, minds, and wallets.

Mobile is continuing to become a larger part in the day-to-day lives of consumers. Free-time, downtime, lunch breaks, social situations, shopping, etc. these are places where you can spot people spending some time on mobile devices. Anytime and anyplace can become the casual setting to pull out a phone. Mobile devices have outdone just about every other electronic gadget hands-down.

If you are a business owner, this means that you need a mobile-friendly website in order to capitalize on the millions of web searches performed by mobile phone users.

People don't leave home without their cell phones and more and more people today use them to search for businesses while on the go. But what if your business has a website that can't be viewed properly on mobile devices?

Some people even have problems finding a phone number on some websites when using their mobile devices. Mobile users typically just want basic information when searching for a business on their mobile device, so mobile websites are made to be easy to navigate and use very few text and graphics.

If your business offers products or services to consumers, it is in your best interest to make sure they are able to view your website on their mobile devices. For instance, restaurants, stores, coffee shops, movie theaters, and dry cleaners, just to name a few. Everyone should consider investing into a mobile-friendly website.

For example, if you are a restaurant, the most important thing for consumers to see on your website is your phone number. If they are using their mobile device to try to find you, then they're probably looking to call you to make reservations.

In short, consumers who search their mobile devices for businesses will usually go with those who have a mobile-friendly website. Trying to navigate a regular site on a mobile device is a big headache. So if your potential customer can't immediately find what they need, they move on to the next one!

Get the edge on your competitors and get a mobile website so you can be located easily by mobile users.

Important Mobile Facts

When a potential customer has a bad mobile experience with your website it can cost you money!

- 9 out of 10 mobile searches lead to action. More than 50% lead to sales.

- 81% of smart phone users have done product research from a smart phone, and 50% have made a purchase via their phone.

- 57% of users say they won't recommend a business with a poorly designed mobile site.

- 60% of users expect a mobile site to load in three seconds or less.

- Google says 61% of users are unlikely to return to a mobile site they had trouble accessing and 40% visit a competitor's site instead.

- 88% of consumers who search for a type of local business on a mobile device call or go to that business within 24 hours.

- 71% of users expect a mobile site to load as fast as a desktop site.

- Average smart phone conversion rates are up 64% compared to the average desktop conversion rates.

- 74% of people use their mobile phone to help them while shopping, with 79% making a purchase as a result.

- Mobile coupons receive 10x higher redemption rates than print coupons.

- 33% of U.S. mobile users prefer offers via text to mobile Web 21%, Apps 11% and voice mail 8%.

- 73% of smart phone users say they used the mobile web to make a purchase instead of using an app.

- 95% of smart phone users have used their phone to look up local information. After doing so, 61% called, and 59% visited.

- 50% of survey respondents report responding to a text offer. Of that same group, 32% have scanned a coupon via a QR code.

- When asked why they would scan a QR code, 87% of smart phone users said it was to access a coupon, discount or deal.

- 16% of smart phone users have made a purchase because of a marketing message they received on a phone. And half of those who purchased made the purchase from the smart phone itself.

- 64% of decision-makers read their e-mail via mobile devices.

Why Your Business Should Cash-In On Mobile Marketing

Everyone knows that TV commercials, newspapers, radio ads, and other traditional advertising methods are losing their effectiveness. Therefore, businesses are looking for new ways to put a twist on their marketing methods. This is one of the reasons why mobile advertising is rapidly increasing in popularity as a "must-have" marketing tool. Mobile marketing allows businesses to reach their target audiences easily and more effortless than other marketing methods. Not only that, but mobile marketing has also proven to be extremely effective in producing a higher ROI when it comes to your marketing efforts. There are BILLIONS of mobile phone users worldwide. Mobile devices are more heavily used than the traditional PC. In fact, mobile devices are practically a permanent attachment for most people today. Are you starting to see the power in mobile marketing? You can literally reach your potential market no matter where they are because they will have their mobile device right by their sides!

The 3 top Internet search engines – Google, Yahoo, and Microsoft – have` made great strides to capitalize on the massive mobile device usage by consumers today. They all have created mobile platforms for Internet browsing and advertising. Advertising over a mobile phone provides the ability to reach a massive number of people as many of them are now browsing the web using their mobile devices.

As you can see, mobile marketing is really just getting started and is already ON FIRE. This means that your business needs to be a part of this revolution to boost your profits.

Now is the time for you to break into the very lucrative area of mobile marketing! Competition is lower than any other advertising method as most businesses have not caught on just yet – but they will. However, businesses that are taking action RIGHT NOW have the upper hand as they are claiming their mobile ground before their competitors do.

What Exactly Is Mobile Marketing?

A lot of people think of mobile marketing as simply a way for businesses to advertise to people via their cell phones.

While this may have been true years ago, mobile marketing encompasses much more than that today.

Mobile marketing can be considered an umbrella of many different mobile services available today that can help businesses bring in new customers and repeat customers. In fact, it has never been easier to reach your target audience!

Everyone is aware that one of the most effective ways to push content to consumers is through the Internet. However, mobile marketing allows you to be even more interactive with your prospects and customers.

Think about the number of people who own cell phones… Think about the number of people who don't leave home without their cell phones… It's pretty apparent that people are pretty much tied to their cell phones these days. So mobile marketing allows you to capitalize on this fact and increase your profits along the way.

Mobile marketing consists of several different methods of advertising such as:

- **Mobile Websites** – Most cell phones don't have full Internet browsers that will allow them to view regular web pages. Therefore, businesses are creating mobile versions of their website so they can be easily viewed on mobile devices. This is important as many people are now using their smart phones to access business websites. Imagine one of your potential customers not being able to see your phone number or address on your website when they pull it up on their phone; it is money lost. If your website is not mobile friendly visit www.OnTargetMarketingGroup.com we have a powerful solution to make your existing website mobile friendly. We can also create a fresh mobile friendly site built for converting leads to customers. To check and see if your website is mobile friendly visit www.google.com/webmasters/tools/mobile-friendly/

- **SMS (Short Message Service)** – This allows you to send text messages out to your customers to notify them of any specials or promotions you may have going on. In short, it is an easy way to keep your existing customers coming back to buy from you over and over again.

- **QR Codes (Quick Response Codes)** - QR codes are 2 dimensional bar codes that are used to transfer information through mobile phone barcode readers. You can have a QR code created for your business and then put it on all of your marketing materials, including your business cards, flyers, and website just to name a few. Once you have a QR code, smart phone users can scan it and automatically be directed to your website, to a promotional offer, or wherever you want them to go. This powerful form of mobile technology is becoming more and more popular and businesses all over the world are jumping on board.

    When it comes to marketing your business, mobile marketing allows you to tap into your target audience easily and effectively. But once you understand the basics and see the power in it, you too will start leveraging this profit-boosting technology!

Text Messaging

EMobile devices have pretty much become a permanent human attachment. Because of this, text messaging is at an all-time high. Most people prefer texting than picking up the phone to call someone. It's quick, convenient, and effective.

Businesses can capitalize on this frenzy and easily reach their prospective customers by simply building a list of mobile subscribers. Once your customers subscribe, you can send them short promotional messages that will bring them back to purchase from you again.

Let's look at 5 reasons why SMS text marketing is so effective:

1. Personalized communication.

SMS text marketing allows you to continuously communicate with your customers through a form of personal communication. Unlike traditional marketing methods that speak to everyone, your text messages help give you that personal touch with your customer-base. It has been proven that any form of "personalized" marketing is much more effective than general marketing tactics.

2. Targeted Marketing

Unlike other forms of advertisement that target a wide range of people, mobile marketing allows you to target your customers directly. This form of marketing is instrumental in turning your existing customers into loyal, long-term customers. Therefore, you are able to boost your profits without spending more money on advertising.

3. Affordable

Short message service (SMS), also known as "text messaging" has proven to be ten times more effective than other advertising tools, including mail and newspaper advertising. Many of today's mobile marketing plans are very affordable, and with such a small price, you can realize huge returns in no time. You can also save more money by using discounted plans.

4. High Response Rates

The average response rates for mobile marketing campaigns are around 15%. This is around five times higher than the average email marketing campaign. Higher response rates mean a higher ROI for your marketing budget.

5. Easily Trackable

Mobile marketing is simple to track thanks to technology. In most cases, you will be able to track how many people opened your message and how many people acted on your message. Can you track any of this with a newspaper or Yellow pages ad?

As you can see, there are many benefits to mobile marketing that can help you increase profits in your business. It's effective, affordable, targeted, and very easy to track.

Businesses today are realizing the power in this form of marketing and are jumping on the bandwagon. Mobile marketing is the newest wave of digital technology that will allow you to out-do your competitors with very little time, money, and effort.

Five Mobile Marketing Mistakes to AVOID

1. Treating Mobile Users Like PC Users

Unlike PC users, mobile users don't want to download

your entire seven-page report. Instead, they are looking for fast access to information since they are usually on the move. Mobile users are not interested in doing a lot of clicking around to get what they need. So your information should be exact with very few words, images and graphics.

2. Not "Targeting" An Audience

Mobile marketing with text messages only works when you send the message to the right people. Some companies make the mistake of treating SMS (Short Message Service) like a mass marketing media instead of the targeting tool it was meant to be.

Text marketing campaigns allow you to use specific demographic and behavioral information to target specific consumer groups at specific times. "Targeting" means your message is highly relevant to consumers, which results in a more successful campaign overall.

To get the best use of mobile marketing, be sure to properly target your potential market.

3. Hard-Selling Using SMS

Mobile is a great way to interact with consumers, but if all of your communication with them is hard-selling, chances are you will lose most of your subscribers. Many companies make the mistake of bombarding consumers with hard sales pitches that add no value to the consumer.

Some send constant messages about irrelevant new products and some push the same services over and over until they become a pure annoyance.

Don't become one of them. Instead, you want to provide

value to your customers through your mobile marketing campaigns. If consumers feel like they are benefiting from the text marketing relationship they'll accept and embrace it. If not, your efforts could potentially damage your brand.

4. Using Mobile Marketing Alone

While mobile marketing campaigns are effective when used on their own, they pack even more power when they are used as part of an overall marketing strategy. If you are using online marketing, email marketing, or even TV ads and newspaper ads, mobile marketing can be a perfect fit to integrate into those methods.

For instance, you can use short codes in your call to action in TV ads, radio ads, and newspapers. Not only that, but you can even add your business's QR (Quick Response Code) to your other advertising campaigns. Consumers can scan your QR code with their cell phones and be taken right to your website, receive an instant coupon, or even take a virtual tour of your business!

5. Using One-Way SMS Marketing

Mobile marketing is a great way to communicate back and forth with consumers, but most businesses use it as a boring one-way communication channel. What a huge mistake! Mobile marketing is an easy way to connect with consumers instead of just "sell" to them.

Your list will appreciate this more and feel like you are building a relationship with them. Once they "like" and "trust" you, that's when they'll start buying from you.

For instance, you can interact with them by asking them to

text in an idea for something related to your business. They will feel more engaged and will be more receptive to all of your marketing messages if you mix it up a bit and let them talk back to you.

Why Are QR Codes Important For Your Business?

QR (Quick Response) codes are two-dimensional bar codes that are regularly used in conjunction with mobile phones to gain quick access to websites amongst other things.

How do they work?

QR codes are 2 dimensional bar codes that are used to transfer information through barcode readers that can be found on most mobile devices. Anyone with a camera phone (some may require a bar-code reader) can scan a business's QR code and one of several things can happen:

1. They will be taken to their website.

2. They will be sent a coupon or discount.

3. The business's contact information will be instantly stored on their phone.

4. There are many other options of what can happen once they scan the code – the choice is yours.

QR Codes provide instant gratification with consumers, which is one reason that they are becoming more and more popular in the marketing world. There are some successful campaigns that had engagement rates of up to 60%, which far exceeds normal direct-mail response rates.

One of the most attractive features of QR codes, from a

business standpoint, is that you can change the content delivered via your QR code pretty much on the fly. Today, you may want to offer a 20% off coupon to all consumers who scan your QR code. Tomorrow, you may want the code to provide consumers with a quick tutorial on how to use your product.

You're in luck… unlike print advertising, QR code content can be quickly and easily changed to promote whatever you want – whenever you want. They can also provide additional information, like where your product can be purchased, that can be key to gaining new customers and increasing your market share.

So as you can see, QR codes provide a lot of options for businesses and almost any business can find a way to take advantage of them. Whether you are promoting a product or a special service, incorporating an interactive QR code will give you a new way to get the attention of your target audience.

5 Ways to Use QR Codes in Your Business

QR codes make it easy for Smartphone users to scan codes to get information about your business rather than having to send a text message, make a call, or wait until they get home to look at your website. This makes your advertising job a whole lot easier as it requires minimum effort on your part to get this accomplished.

Just to give you some ideas about the power of QR codes, here are 5 ways to use them in your business:

1. Use your QR code on your Google Places Local Business listing page. Google has already setup a QR code for you if you have a brick and mortar business. All you need to do is log into your account and download it and you're done! When someone comes across your Google Places Local

Business listing page, they can scan your code and instantly save your information to their mobile device.

2. Use your QR code on your website. When visitors visit your site, make sure your QR code is completely visible so they can easily swipe it and save all of your information to their mobile device. Not only that, but make sure it is on your Facebook Fanpage as well.

3. Use your QR code on your printed marketing materials. Your flyers, brochures, business cards, and anything else you use to market your business should have your QR code printed on it as well. If you advertise on billboards or TV, you can put them there too.

4. Use your QR code to build a list of mobile subscribers by using mobile keywords and short codes. For instance, you can run an advertising campaign telling consumers to text "special234" to receive 20% off your products or services. Once they send the text message, they are instantly subscribed to your list. Once they are on your list, you can promote additional offers and build relationships with them going forward.

5. Use multiple QR codes for different activities and promotions within your business. For instance, if you want to offer a coupon for 10%, create a QR code for it and promote it. If you want to share customer testimonials and reviews, create a QR code for it and promote it. If you want to share information about your newest product that is launching, create a QR code for it and promote it.

These are just a few things you can do with a custom QR code. They can be used online, at your physical location, on your direct mail pieces, and many other ways as you can see. They are perfect for your marketing arsenal when it comes to promoting specials offers, videos, product launches, and pretty much any other promotional effort. The possibilities are endless.

Conclusion

Mobile marketing is a proven way to increase revenue to your business. It is imperative as a business owner you understand the power of mobile marketing and take advantage of this opportunity. Building a strong relationship with your customers using text message and QR codes will prove to be very fruitful in the days ahead. And, if your website is not mobile friendly you could be losing out on tons of potential mobile customers.

Now is the time to build a mobile marketing strategy.

CHAPTER 10

WORKING SMARTER, NOT HARDER

Online marketing, like any marketing, is multi-faceted and requires a great amount of work, coupled with a hefty learning curve for those who have never done it before. Today's online marketing requires a lot more expertise and maintenance than previously. For instance, monitoring your Web 2.0 applications should be checked daily. This one area can eat up precious time in your schedule and even take more time if you don't know what you are doing. It will behoove many business owners to outsource their online marketing to experts. There is too much at stake to leave anything undone or done incorrectly.

By outsourcing your online local marketing, you can ensure your online marketing is done by those who are skilled in the field.

You can conserve your own time to spend on the tasks in your company that rely on your skill sets. In addition, the implementation of your marketing changes (which are necessary to effect a change in your sales), will get done quicker than if you had to learn how to do it yourself.

Most business owners are spending 80+ hours weekly in their business, doing the things necessary to be successful. These people are the masters of their domains and know what they are doing in their field of expertise. However, taking extraordinary amounts of time to learn and master internet marketing does not always make sense or come easy.

What does make sense is for them to continue doing the things they know how to do well and let a professional in internet marketing take care of that side of the equation for them. This is time and resources well spent.

Time is a crucial factor when you think about marketing your business. With the help of a professional internet marketer, your business can easily rank #1 in Google searches for local keywords very quickly. By ranking number you can experience a stampede of new leads.

If you were to do it yourself, where would you be in the process of implementing your online business plan? Would you still be learning, procrastinating or would you actually have things done? Do you have the time to devote to this?

The Power of Outsourcing

Outsourcing Can Take Care of:

- Site design
- Sales Funnels

- Landing pages for PPC campaigns
- Content Creation
- Video creation (slide show style)
- Video marketing
- Article marketing
- Directory submissions
- SEO & Backlink generation
- PPC campaign management
- Social networking setup
- Email marketing setup
- General marketing consultant
- Mobile marketing

In each of these categories there are so many more tasks which must be mastered before implementing them effectively on your website and in your overall marketing strategy. By hiring a professional, all aspects can be taken care of quickly and easily.

With the strategic marketing points found in this book you can easily work with your internet marketing company to create an effective game plan together that will meet your company goals. You are no longer in the dark! You have now been given a manual to help guide you to unlocking internet lead success.

Let's take a closer look at each marketing category below.

Site Design

This can be much more than just creating a site from scratch. Internet marketers can also do any of the following:

- Site Cleanup
- Meta tag cleanup
- Total redesign
- Setup contact forms
- Add audio
- Add video
- Mobile friendly website

Landing Pages for PPC

Internet marketers can help you setup a landing page that:

- Has proper keyword density
- Has an opt-in or capture page for collecting emails to be used later

Content Creation

There is a wide range of services an internet marketer can handle:

- Website content
- Blog writing

- Article writing
- Email messages
- Free giveaway report
- Capture page writing
- Press release writing

Video Creation

This can be done in the form of a Slideshow or even live action. Here, they can create videos for:

- Your website
- Capture pages
- Off-site properties
- Video marketing

Video Marketing

Just what it sounds like, this is marketing with video. This can be done by:

- Submitting to video sharing sites
- Repurpose for multiple keywords
- Submit to external blogs
- Submit to social media sites and business directories

Article Marketing

Some internet marketers and article writing services can:

- Ghostwrite your articles for publication
- Write to submit to article directories
- Position for branding and backlinks

Directory Submissions

This is the key for any business and can be done by:

- Submitting to top directories
- Submitting to local directories
- Submitting to niche directories
- Manage an Advice Local or Yext account
- Pick a number of directories they will submit your site to per month

SEO & Backlink Generation

Get your website ranked higher in the search engines by:

- On-Page optimization
- Off-Page optimization
- Diversified and quality backlinks galore

PPC Campaign Management

They manage your PPC campaigns with:

- Google AdWords
- Yahoo sponsored search
- Microsoft Ad Center

- Lesser known PPC spots
- Facebook Ads
- YouTube Ads
- Navigator Ads

Social Networking Setup

This is becoming more and more popular these days and with this they can:

- Set up profiles on Facebook, Twitter, Linked In, and more
- Develop existing profiles
- Tweak backgrounds
- Add content
- Create groups
- Add friends / followers

Email Marketing Setup

Internet marketers can help you capture emails and use those emails to:

- Send giveaway reports
- Setup capture pages
- Setup auto-responders
- Write a series of emails
- Create drip marketing email campaigns

General Marketing Consultant

The sky's the limit here and marketers can provide you with:

- Anything that will improve your business
- Internet Marketing Consulting
- Give you guidance and instructions on setting up any of the other business tactics from above.

Mobile Marketing

- SMS marketing
- Mobile friendly website
- Mobile SEO

In addition to any or all of these tasks, a skilled internet marketer can become your online marketing partner, doing all your internet marketing tasks for you on a continuity bases. This makes you essentially completion proof, because there is someone staying on top of everything for you and constantly getting more and more links and ranking for you for more and more keywords. It's a win-win situation.

Choosing the Right Outsourcers

If you decide subcontracting your online marketing out to another firm is the right decision for you, take the time to find the right subcontractor. You should begin by deciding what you want done for you and what you plan to do yourself. It is fine to let a subcontractor do everything for you.

Next find an online marketer who is an authority in the field.

Good choices are those individuals who make presentations for business groups on the topic of *internet marketing*. Other good choices are those who appear at the top of natural local searches for internet marketers, because this means they can actually do what they say they can do.

If an online marketer is everywhere, including in the top several spots on searches, you can feel confident he or she is a leader in the field and a good choice for you.

There are so many different internet marketers who offer some or all of the things above. Some specialize in just one area, while others offer all online marketing services.

You need to determine if you want to take care of any of the tasks yourself, with an employee or through a professional. Internet marketers will often provide a variety of options for you to choose from to tailor the service you are purchasing to your needs.

A La Carte

This is ideal for those who want to keep a handle on things and have a good knowledge of some of the areas of internet marketing. It also works well for those who want to learn some of the specialties mentioned here.

Package Deals

This is the perfect solution for the busy local business person who does not have the time or interest in learning the details of internet marketing. It allows for quicker implementation of all the different parts of internet marketing (as there is no learning curve involved). Those who will be doing your internet marketing already know what they are doing. You just need to prepare for the influx of new business.

Purchasing Leads

There are companies out there who have done all the internet marketing in your domain and have the Web 2.0 applications in place. They have gathered leads for the type of products and services you deal in. You can simply purchase leads from such companies and follow up on them yourself.

Continuity Programs

With the purchase of a continuity program, you have an internet marketer on retainer. These individuals offer programs whereby they implement new marketing strategies monthly over a fixed period of time, or they do all the implementation of the strategies at the beginning, and simply maintain them over a given period of time.

In each of these categories there are so many more tasks that must be mastered before implementing them effectively on your website. By hiring a professional, all aspects are taken care of quickly and easily.

CHAPTER 11

PUTTING IT ALL TOGETHER

Your online marketing strategy is based on getting more qualified visitors to your site and converting them into leads, enquiries, sales or customers. It really is that simple!

Through using a wide variety of techniques you can pinpoint those customers and make sure they find your business when they search online for products or services you provide. When they find your website a variety of other online marketing tools will be waiting to convert them into buying customers. To do this effectively, most of your focus will be on 2 major aspects of your marketing plan.

First, you'll use keywords in all online content and creating as many links as possible to your website. The more backlinks you have, the better your site will place in the search engine results and the more people will find your website. The more effectively you use keywords, the more search engine friendly your content is and therefore more likely to be ranked.

Second, the more visitors you get to your website, the more new customers you will create for your services or products. New customers mean an increase in sales and profits.

Techniques to Increase Your Business's Profits

Whether you have suffered a downturn in your business, have never built it to the level were aiming for, or if you are just starting out, your goal needs to be using online marketing strategies to increase your profits.

There are Three Basic Ways to Improve Profits:

1) **Increase Customers**
   - Increase traffic to increase customers.
   - Add to product offerings to make them more compelling.
   - Use PPC, SEO, local business results, article marketing etc.

2) **Increase number of transactions per customer**
   - Build mailing list.
   - Increase customer communications through autoresponders, newsletters, broadcast messages.
   - Offer them up sell opportunities – pitch something special.
   - Send out reminders for services and specials.

3) **Increase the average dollar amount per transactions**

- Offer bundle packages and upgrades, strong reasons to purchase.
- Decrease costs, finding free traffic, lowering cost per click.
- Increasing conversions, decreases costs.
- Offer a bonus, change a headline or offer a free consultation.
- Even converting from 1% to 2% is a 100% improvement and cuts costs for buying traffic in half – Pure profit!.

By putting an online marketing plan in place and following through with it, you can achieve all of these goals.

You can easily improve your profits through the strategic use of online marketing techniques that will increase customers, increase the number of transactions per customer, increase the average dollar amount per transaction and decrease costs while finding free traffic; which leads to a lower cost per click.

Take the time today to investigate if your website is doing all it can do to attract new clients for you. If not, get started putting the simple online marketing plan into place on your own or with the help of a professional.

Get started now on your online marketing plan to rescue your business.

CHAPTER 12

ONE LAST MESSAGE

Your online marketing strategy is based on your ongoing ability to stay ahead of your competition. Once you've made your presence known on the World Wide Web it's up to you to keep the momentum going.

You defined goals and objectives for your website the moment you gave birth to it. Your product or services grow and expand your business based on your performance. It's as simple as Business 101.

The activity of leading your website to the top of the search engines is in your hands. You are constantly:

- Leading
- Directing
- Motivating
- Actuating
- Much More…

It's easier to understand complex management of your website or websites when you see it mapped out in steps. This is what this book is about. It's a tool to assist you in organization, in designing and developing a step-by-step plan to get your website to center page rank #1 in all the major search engines.

Your business isn't on an efficient assembly-line in a factory. Your product or service is sold over cyberspace. Yet, how you sell your product or service does not lessen your need to approach your market in a straightforward, powerful way. You must have the ability to determine what your plan of action is in regard to marketing, and you must stick to the plan.

It's hard work. No one said it was going to happen overnight. Yet, if you set a good standard of performance for your online business presence and you work toward the goals you've set as your established standards, then you can't help but to succeed.

If you continually follow the guidelines presented throughout this book you can't go wrong. You can only go wrong if you're not putting in the hours, working your internet plan, following through with your customers, steadily growing your customer-base, and expanding your business. That's how you make the money online.

Take the time now to review if your website is being as effective as it can be to get new leads, customers or sales. If not, now is the time to implement a new plan either by following the steps in this book or with the help of a professional online marketing services provider.

"Successful online marketing campaigns quickly build trust where customers want to buy from you. Strategically positioning yourself online will cause you to stand out from the competition and attract more buying customers."

Author Bios

Mike Driggers, is a breakthrough strategist who inspires, motivates, and encourages people worldwide. Mike is recognized as one of the worlds most requested marketing consultants. He is a in demand international celebrity business and motivational keynote speaker who has delivered over 2000+ presentations.

Mike is the author of several books titled *"Mastering of The Mind Set"*, *"Unleashing The Intrapenuer"*, *"1099 Attitude Vs The W2 Way"*, *"Nothing in LIFE Starts Until YOU Start"*, *"Nothing in SALES Starts Until YOU Start"* and *"Nothing in LEADERSHIP Starts Until YOU Start"*.

Mike has also co-authored several books titled *"Entrepreneurs On Fire"* with Barbara Corcoran from the hit TV series, The Shark Tank, *"Your Extraordinary Greatness"* with James Malinchak from the featured hit ABC TV Show Secret Millionaire", "*On Target Marketing*" with Vince Baker co-owner of On Target Marketing Group, and "Managing Your Commitment" with Rick Chavez Sports News Caster

. Mike has owned and operated several very successful businesses, including a Bay Area marketing and advertising agency called Unleashed Media where In 2004, he was voted entrepreneur of the year in his local area by President Bush.

He has been featured on ABC, NBC, CBS, PBS, USA Today, Business Journal, and the Wall Street Journal. Mike has also been in the top 10% of producers for the direct sales industry for more than 25 years.

Mike currently co-owns On Target Marketing Group, and is the owner of IME Publishing. He uses a no-nonsense, highly-focused and disciplined approach to creating real results quickly. He covers subjects including entrepreneurship, mindset, leadership, sales, marketing, high performance and motivation. Mike's passion, desire, and willingness to be a servant leader has inspired and helped thousands of people achieve greatness within their personal and business lives.

As a consultant Mike's is a behind-the-scenes, go-to sales, marketing and leadership advisor for many businesses. His clientele is a Who's Who in the fields of sports, business, entertainment and politics. He has helped people from all walks of life create amazing results quickly and hit top ranks within their business and careers. For more Information and to learn more about Mike go to

www.SuccessWithMikeDriggers.com

Vince W Baker is a highly motivated Internet Marketing Coach, Public Speaker and Author. He is a professional who thrives in multi-dimensional markets. He has a proven track record of succeeding in competitive sales markets, internet marketing, leadership roles and problem solving.

Vince loves working with positive successful teams of people who are goal orientated.

It was with a popular Internet Service Provider where Vince had his first real level of success. In this business he broke multiple company records.

From there he moved into the Yellow Page industry where he quickly produced results and brought in four times more new business than his colleagues. He was quickly promoted to sales manager where he continued outselling and superseded company goals.

Vince was highly sought out and entered into the direct mail business and within a short amount of time became the top sales person bringing in hundreds of new accounts.

During this time Vince saw a huge opportunity to increase business contacts and sales thru the internet and email marketing. He then started his own marketing company and became an industry leader in Internet Marketing, and direct sales thru social media. At this time you could find Vince publicly speaking on a regular basis to business professionals on how to increase their business online.

Vince was one of the first pioneers to forward the Social Media phenomenon within the business community.

Vince has also successfully managed hundreds of people and through coaching, motivation, training, creating manuals, tracking, implementation and direction advanced his teams to the forefront winning multiple achievements in the face of difficult obstacles.

Vince enjoys advising business owners with creative solutions. He has an eye for quickly developing strategies both online and in a competitive business environment to bring success in his areas of expertise. Through his professional approach he is an established asset to any company he works with. For more information and to learn more about Vince go to www.VinceWBaker.com

A **FREE** Gift For **YOU!**
Gain Access To Step-By-Step Training To Unlock The Power Of Internet Marketing!

DOWNLOAD NOW!
www.OnTargetMarketing.com/Giveaways

INSTANT AUTHORITY

Special **FREE** Bonus Gift For **YOU!**

To help you stand out from the crowd **FREE BONUS RESOURCES** for you at;
www.InstantAuthorityNow.com

Get your 3 FREE in-depth training videos sharing how you gain trust from prospective customers. This trust will lead to establishing you as an authority, increase web traffic, boost business sales and attract more referrals. You will also learn how to earn the respect in your industry which can lead to more lucrative partnerships.

www.InstantAuthorityNow.com

CREATIVE MARKETING
AFFORDABLE PRICING
QUICK TURN AROUND

- Internet Marketing
- Business Coaching
- Book Publishing
- Sales Funnels
- Squeeze Pages
- Web Design
- Business Directories
- Social Media Marketing
- Pay-Per-Click
- Webinar Marketing
- Video Marketing
- Email Marketing
- Analytics
- Mobile Marketing
- Graphic Design
- E-Commerce
- Mobile App
- Reputation Management
- Seminar Marketing

Visit Us At
www.OnTargetMarketingGroup.com

THE IDEAL PROFESSIONAL SPEAKERS FOR YOUR NEXT EVENT!

Any organization that wants to develop and grow their business to become "extraordinary" needs to hire Mike or Vince for keynote or workshop training!

TO BOOK MIKE OR VINCE TO SPEAK:

On Target Marketing Group
(925) 222-5037
www.OnTargetMarketingGroup.com

TheOTMGroup@gmail.com

CREATE A STAMPEDE OF LOCAL LEADS
"Share This Book"

Retail 24.95
Special Quantity Discounts

5-20 Books	22.95
21-99 Books	19.95
100-499 Books	15.95
500-999 Books	10.95
1,000 + Books	8.95

To Order Go To www.OnTargetMarketing.com

NOTES:

www.ingramcontent.com/pod-product-compliance
Lightning Source LLC
Chambersburg PA
CBHW071427160426
43195CB00013B/1834